The Path to Heaven

Emily Minjun Chung

THE PATH TO HEAVEN

PERFEX BOOKS LTD., BC, Canada.

ISBN: 978-1-0695600-0-1

First Edition

Prologue
What is Faith?

Faith is a belief that holds steady through both poverty and prosperity, in sickness and in health.

Faith is a realm in which one finds sweetness even in muddy paths and meets despair with a serene smile.

Faith inspires us to give of ourselves generously for the sake of others, enabling us to overcome fear—even the fear of life and death itself.

Because those who hold faith believe that beyond this life lies heaven, a place where their souls will finally rest in peace. But where exactly is this heaven? Perhaps it arrives tomorrow, or maybe it's hidden within today. It might be somewhere high above, or perhaps right here among us.

This is a tale of searching for heaven, that paradise of faith . . .

CHILDREN . OF . A . COMMON . MOTHER

At the inauguration ceremonies of U.S. presidents, they place their hands upon the Bible while taking the oath, clearly showing that they are people of faith. Faith is like a seed planted within the heart, and even more, it is a spiritual legacy. Can we also plant such a seed of faith in our children's hearts?

On the West Coast of North America, in the border park shared by Canada and the United States, stands a structure built over two centuries ago—the Peace Arch. Inscribed upon it are these words: *Children of a Common Mother.*

Some might say that this is simply history from over two hundred years ago. But we must understand that humanity's existence is inherently about passing down traditions and legacies. Some people and events must always be remembered, because when we choose to abandon our history, we also lose our future.

Contents

Chapter 1

Autumn winds lifted fallen leaves into the air. In a quiet corner of a cemetery, Lucas stood silently, as though feeling some mysterious connection with the earth beneath him. Rays of sunlight filtered gently through gaps in the clouds, scattered and fragmented, each beam like grains of sand trickling softly through time, brushing gently against his face. Yet the chilly breeze seemed to remind him of time's relentless passing.

Although the years had carved deep lines into his face, his eyes still shone like stars polished by countless storms—sparkling with a love for life and boundless curiosity for the unknown.

Lucas's hair was streaked with silver, each strand weathered by the passage of time. Yet he still combed it carefully and neatly, revealing a calmness beyond worldly concerns. Gently, he lifted the medical report in his hand—a quiet verdict of fate, announcing that the sunset of his life was slowly slipping below the horizon.

Now, as dawn chased away the shadows of the clouds, the faint, tranquil smile on Lucas's lips lent him a gentle glow as he stood before the gravestone. At that moment, a powerful longing rose within him—a deep and heartfelt yearning to reunite with his beloved.

He murmured softly, his voice like a gentle breeze stirring fallen leaves and caressing the tips of grass. Gazing tenderly at the photograph of his wife, Manon, on the gravestone, he smiled softly and whispered, "My dear, seven years have passed since you left me, and yet every week I still come here to visit you. Our daughter keeps urging me to return to the States; she says I'm growing old, and she wants me near so she can take care of me. But how could she—someone who's never desired marriage—truly understand that I simply cannot bear to leave the place where your soul rests? Ever since you asked to be buried here, beside your parents, my heart has remained forever in Paris.

"Our first meeting, our first embrace and kiss—they all happened here in Paris. Though you lived with me in the States for thirty years, you ultimately chose to return here. Perhaps this was God's plan all along, that our love began here and would continue here. Yes, continue. I've always been afraid you might forget me, so I never dared leave this city. Every week, I come to remind you of your promise—that we will surely meet again in heaven.

"And I promised you in return that I would live well, carrying your blessings with me, and sharing them with everyone I meet. I've kept my word; I stayed in Paris and became a private tour driver, introducing visitors from all over the world to the beauty and romance of this city, enchanting them with your hometown, and blessing them along the way."

The slowly rising autumn sun-bathed the entire cemetery in a gentle warmth, as if each soft ray was carrying Manon's tender affection and loving memories for Lucas.

He spoke softly, "My dear, at most, in one year's time, we'll be reunited in heaven. I'm truly sorry to have left you waiting alone for these past seven years. But please believe me—in this limited journey of time, I will continue to cherish every moment, sharing your blessings with as many people as possible. When I finally leave here to join you again, they too will bless us in return.

"Oh, by the way, our daughter Georgia has become an influencer with millions of followers; she's more than capable of taking care of herself now. I've decided not to tell her about my current health condition. I believe, now that she's in her thirties, she'll eventually find someone who loves her as deeply as we love her, someone who will stay by her side and give her the wonderful life she deserves."

In this moment, Lucas's heart felt like a delicately woven brocade—intertwined with the joy of reuniting with his beloved and the tender sorrow of parting from his daughter, painting an intricate picture of emotions beyond words. He stood quietly before his wife's grave as the gentle breeze brushed past, seemingly carrying away a lingering trace of sadness within him. Gazing tenderly at the photo of his wife on the gravestone, his eyes filled with warmth and deep affection.

"My dear, our daughter has grown into a remarkable woman. Her life is filled with sunshine and hope. Not only does she have millions of devoted followers, becoming a highly admired influencer, but she also shines brightly on the world stage with her unique charm and talent."

In Lucas's heart, Georgia was the precious treasure he and his wife had brought into this world. Independent, resilient, and confident, their daughter never backed down from life's challenges, always greeting each new day with optimism. Each chapter of her growth unfolded like scenes from a beautiful movie, filled with laughter and touching moments. As an influencer, she not only won the affection of countless followers, but had also become Lucas's greatest pride. Warmth filled his heart every time he thought of her. And every single time, with pride and affection, he would share these same thoughts with his wife.

After bidding farewell to Manon, Lucas slowly walked away from the quiet, serene cemetery. His steps were calm and steady as he headed toward the black sedan that had accompanied him faithfully for years. The autumn sunlight, soft as golden silk, gently bathed him, stretching his shadow long upon the ground—a silhouette that appeared both solitary and comforting.

He opened the car door and settled into the seat, gently running his fingers over the steering wheel. Its solid touch felt like the reassuring embrace of an old friend, offering him warmth and solace. He slowly closed the car door, as if quietly drawing a curtain between him and the world he'd left behind. He rolled down the window slightly, breathing deeply, allowing the fresh air to fill his chest. With a soft turn of the key, the engine came to life, its deep, steady hum breaking the silence as the car gently pulled away from this peaceful place. As the wheels turned slowly forward, the scenery around him gradually faded from sight, like a river in the early morning Parisian light—profound, serene, and stretching endlessly ahead.

Lucas enjoyed weaving through the charming streets of Paris, encountering tourists from all corners of the globe. Each conversation felt like destiny, offering him opportunities to listen to diverse stories and share reflections on life. Through his storytelling, the beautiful sights of Paris were transformed from mere static images into vivid, vibrant scenes, gracefully unfolding before his passengers' eyes. The city's historical anecdotes, cultural heritage, and artistic treasures came alive through his words, captivating and enchanting everyone who listened.

Just as Lucas was immersed in the gentle flow of his thoughts, savoring this precious moment of tranquility, a sudden ringtone rippled clearly through the silence, gently pulling him back to reality. Calmly, he answered via the car's Bluetooth connection, and a young woman's voice filled the car, informing him that her flight had just landed at Paris Charles de Gaulle Airport.

She was the client Lucas was scheduled to pick up today; over the next few days, he would be her private driver and tour guide, accompanying her around the city.

This was an assignment originating from the distant East. With this client's arrival, Lucas embarked on his journey to find paradise, and thus, the story gently began to unfold . . .

Chapter 2

At Charles de Gaulle Airport, Lucas parked the car neatly and walked into the arrival hall holding a name card. His timing was impeccable. A gentle breeze brushed through his salt-and-pepper hair, while sunlight danced upon the large glass windows, reflecting shimmering rays like golden threads delicately intertwined at the intersection where glass met floor.

Heading toward him was a young Asian woman, graceful and delicate, seemingly in her early twenties. She passed gracefully through the shimmering threads of sunlight, appearing before Lucas as though emerging from a different dimension.

Quickly regaining his composure, Lucas greeted her with a gentle smile and spoke in English, "Miss Wei, I presume? You can call me Lucas. It's a pleasure to meet you—I'll be your guide, interpreter, and driver during your stay in Paris."

The young woman replied in fluent English, "Thank you, Lucas. My name is Wei Yixin. It's very nice to meet you as well. I don't speak French, so I'll have to rely on your help over the next few days."

Lucas smiled, taking her luggage and guiding her towards the parked car. Apologetically, he mentioned, "I'm sorry, but the parking area is a bit far from here. I noticed that aside from your visit to the Louvre tomorrow, your itinerary doesn't include anything else. Have you made any other plans? If not, I'd be happy to help you arrange something."

The young woman gratefully responded, "Oh, sorry! I'm an artist, and one of my paintings was invited to be exhibited at the Louvre. Tomorrow, I'll meet with their staff and attend this international art exhibition.

Over the next few days, I'd mainly like to view artwork and perhaps meet other artists. Exploring Paris has always been my childhood dream, but unfortunately, I might not have enough time on this trip."

Lucas was genuinely surprised. "Wow, you're an artist?"

The young woman nodded gently, speaking softly, "I'm a product designer as well as an artist. It's an honor to have my work invited to participate in this exhibition. I'm really hoping this visit to Paris will be rewarding."

After placing her luggage in the car, they drove away from the airport. Lucas introduced the surroundings along the way, "The hotel you've booked is near the Louvre. There's a small café nearby that serves an excellent cappuccino. After you check in, I'll wait downstairs. If you'd like, I'd be delighted to treat you to a coffee there."

The young woman smiled warmly. "I'd be honored."

Driving through the streets of Paris, Lucas enthusiastically shared charming anecdotes and historical tales of the city, while the young woman listened quietly, occasionally asking thoughtful questions. With each exchange, their conversation deepened, creating a relaxed and pleasant atmosphere between them.

In the amber glow of an autumn evening, they sat at a small table outside a quaint, uniquely decorated café adorned with vintage lanterns and colorful flags, radiating warmth and romance. Two cups of coffee rested on the table between them as their relaxed and cheerful conversation drifted gently through the evening air, effortlessly moving from personal anecdotes to a lively discussion about the culinary cultures of China and France.

Lucas listened intently, captivated by Wei Yixin's vivid descriptions of the exquisite beauty and rich flavors of Chinese cuisine—the meticulous attention to color, aroma, and taste. In return, Lucas shared insights into French cuisine's elegant plating and refined culinary artistry. Their dialogue naturally evolved into a deeper exploration of the histories and philosophies behind their countries' respective food cultures, highlighting how people from different cultural backgrounds emotionally connect with their meals.

As they discussed plans for visiting the Louvre the following day, Lucas's evident curiosity prompted Wei Yixin to smile warmly and explain, "It's an exclusive, invitation-only art event. However, if you don't mind, you could attend as my translator. That way, you'd have full access to appreciate all the artwork on display."

Lucas responded with a courteous bow, gently expressing his gratitude.

The next morning, they arrived at the Louvre ahead of schedule. As Wei Yixin spoke with the event organizers, Lucas experienced his first taste of such an exclusive art exhibition. He was both amazed and filled with curiosity, thoroughly enjoying the unexpected privilege.

Suddenly noticing that Wei Yixin had vanished from sight, Lucas quickly moved deeper into the exhibition hall, carefully checking each painting's signature along the way, hoping to find traces of her.

Shortly afterward, Lucas's attention was captured by a painting titled *Sunset*, prominently displayed in a central spot. A captivated crowd had gathered around it. Beneath the painting stood Wei Yixin, gracefully smiling as cameras around her captured this unforgettable moment.

Standing quietly at the edge of the crowd, Lucas watched Wei Yixin gracefully handle the attention, patiently responding to reporters' questions. While waiting, Lucas's gaze drifted toward the painting, stirring vivid memories of countless sunsets he had admired through his car window. Those daily scenes—endless rays of intertwined sunlight—felt like gentle caresses from heaven, as if Manon herself were comforting him, warming the remainder of his days with happiness.

Unknowingly, Lucas's eyes began to glisten with tears. Suddenly, a gentle tap on his shoulder brought him back to reality. Wei Yixin had quietly approached him from behind and softly asked, "Are you alright?"

Lucas smiled somewhat awkwardly, replying, "I'm fine. Your painting is incredibly moving—it's truly beautiful. It unintentionally brought back some memories."

As evening descended, the vibrant lights of Paris softly enveloped the beautiful city. At the same charming café as the previous night, Lucas and Wei Yixin enjoyed dessert following dinner and the successful exhibition. Lucas sincerely thanked her for the lovely meal.

Wei Yixin gently laughed and said, "I'm the one who should thank you for your company. Without your translations today, I wouldn't have been able to communicate with so many people. It seems Parisians aren't very fond of speaking English."

Lucas gave a knowing smile, "This is, after all, the great France."

Both shared an understanding laugh. Then, Wei Yixin paused briefly before growing serious and cautiously asking, "Lucas, do you believe in God?"

Lucas answered concisely yet firmly, "Without a doubt, yes."

Wei Yixin hesitated, carefully choosing her words. Noticing she had more to say, Lucas patiently waited, giving her an encouraging look.

She took a deep breath and began slowly, "About half a year ago, I had a dream. I climbed up a hillside, and suddenly saw a grand, majestic church standing on the opposite hilltop. I'm a designer, and I'm certain that such a structure doesn't exist anywhere. Just then, a powerful voice from above echoed in my ears, saying, 'Child, paint this, and show it to the world.' Shocked, I asked, 'What?' The voice replied again, 'You will understand.'"

Lucas softly asked, "Did you paint it?"

Wei Yixin nodded, gently pulling out a neatly folded piece of paper from her bag. As she unfolded it, an exquisitely painted image of a church emerged.

Lucas's eyes widened in astonishment, instantly captivated by the artwork, as if frozen in place. "A miracle!" his heart proclaimed, deeply moved by what he saw.

Wei Yixin continued softly, "This is exactly what I saw in my dream. When I woke up, I immediately painted it. Over the past six months, that voice has kept appearing in my dreams. I'm confused—I've painted it, but I don't know what to do next. I'm afraid that if I share this, people will think I'm strange. So, I wondered if you know anyone from the clergy, or if you could help me find some answers."

Her eyes reflected deep uncertainty as she concluded, "I'm desperately hoping to understand this mysterious dream."

Chapter 3

Lucas gazed at the artwork, his eyes widening with astonishment and awe. Unable to contain his admiration, he exclaimed, "Praise God! If I hadn't seen this painting with my own eyes, your dream would be impossible to believe—truly incredible! I can only imagine the kind of looks I'd receive if I tried to describe your vision to someone else."

The girl replied with an embarrassed smile, "Exactly. It was only after arriving in Europe that I finally dared to speak about it."

Lucas realized that the girl had misunderstood him and quickly clarified, "Miss Wei, what I meant was—I have unwavering faith in my Lord, and I firmly believe that all good souls eventually return to heaven. I was simply praising the greatness of God. Regarding the voice you heard in your dream saying, 'You will understand,' please forgive me, but I don't have the answers either. However, if you have some time, perhaps we could visit the church I regularly attend and speak with our pastor. He might have the insight you're seeking. Oh, and you should know—I'm simply a devout Christian."

The girl broke into a delighted smile. "That's wonderful! Thank you so much, Lucas. This has been troubling me for half a year. Can we visit the church tomorrow?"

Lucas hesitated. "But haven't you forgotten? You still have those art events scheduled for the next two days."

The girl responded with an easy laugh. "True art must come from the soul. For an artist, any opportunity to uplift or enrich the soul is worth pursuing for a lifetime. So, finding the answer to this dream that's been troubling me—there's nothing more important than that."

Lucas nodded understandingly. "No wonder I was so deeply moved when I saw your artwork today—I nearly lost myself for a moment. All right, we'll visit the pastor at the church tomorrow. I'll arrange it in the morning and then come pick you up."

The next morning dawned bright and clear. Lucas hadn't been waiting long outside the hotel where the young artist was staying when he saw her approaching with steps so light and graceful, she seemed almost to be skipping. Smiling warmly, Lucas greeted her cheerfully, "Good morning!" as he gently opened the car door, inviting her inside. She returned his smile, softly lifting the hem of her skirt, and thanked him politely as she settled comfortably into the black seat.

Lucas remarked warmly, "Miss Wei, you must have had a restful night—you look wonderfully refreshed this morning."

She replied brightly, "Yes—I can finally get some answers! Let's go; I can hardly wait."

Their smiles reflected the clear sky above as the car gently pulled away, heading toward the church.

The church stood quietly in a corner of the city, emanating an air of sacred solemnity, bridging the earthly realm to heaven itself. Upon entering, they were greeted by a spacious, luminous hall, the towering dome above rendered even more magnificent by the interplay of sunlight and interior lighting.

Along each side of the hall stood rows of graceful pillars, like loyal guardians silently watching over this sacred space. Intricate carvings adorned their surfaces, each narrating ancient stories, immediately enveloping visitors in an awe-inspiring sense of sanctity and solemnity that transcended time and space.

Ahead, lay the main altar. Towering above it, a majestic statue of Jesus Christ radiated sacred brilliance in the filtered sunlight. His compassionate, blessing eyes seemed capable of soothing all pain and sorrow in the world.

Lucas and the young artist crossed through the main sanctuary and gently opened a side door, stepping into a quiet corner of the church. There, they saw an elderly pastor whose silvery hair shimmered gently under the soft candlelight, illuminated by the wisdom of his many years. His face was kind yet profound, and his eyes radiated tranquility and insight.

Lucas and the girl politely greeted the pastor and introduced themselves. Lucas then began conversing with him in French. Their voices, initially gentle and relaxed, gradually grew more solemn. Although the girl couldn't understand their words, she felt increasingly tense and anxious.

When Lucas asked the girl to present her artwork, she carefully handed it to the pastor, her actions full of reverence and devotion toward the unknown.

In the painting, the church lay draped over the earth like the mantle of God—at once solemn and gentle. Sunlight streamed through its windows, casting warm, sacred patches of light upon pristine white walls, filling the scene with divine grace. The church's spire stretched skyward, guiding humanity toward heaven itself.

The girl watched eagerly as Lucas handed the artwork to the pastor, feeling transported back into her dream. Before her eyes, the church appeared again, gracefully situated upon a hillside at the edge of a small town. Devout believers streamed inside, seeking solace and spiritual guidance. She could almost sense herself standing beside the pulpit, blending this sacred vision deep into her soul through her brush and paints.

The pastor accepted the artwork, glanced at it briefly, and gently shook his head. Turning to Lucas, he spoke in a calm, measured tone, "Lucas, every year countless people come to me claiming they've dreamed of divine miracles. I've been here for more than thirty years, and I've heard endless stories like this. Those dreams, those visions—they're merely reflections of people's inner desires and fantasies projected onto the canvas of the night. Who among us has truly heard the voice of God? We must distinguish clearly between genuine faith and personal obsession."

The pastor's words struck Lucas like icy water, momentarily short-circuiting his thoughts. Confused and taken aback, he instinctively asked, "I'm sorry—I don't understand what you mean."

An expression of weariness and resignation appeared in the pastor's eyes. He furrowed his brow slightly and spoke softly, "I've served the church for many years, Lucas, and never once have I heard God's voice. Dreams like this merely reflect one's inner obsessions. You need to relax—perhaps take a vacation by the sea. Once you've rested and cleared your mind, these dreams and the confusion they cause will naturally resolve themselves."

At last, a trace of compassion surfaced in the

pastor's eyes. He gave Lucas's arm a gentle pat and said, "Lucas, you told me your daughter's waiting for you back in the States. I think you might consider going. Though it's hard, the beauty of life is always there waiting for us. Why not step outside and see for yourself? Well, Lucas, I have other commitments. I wish you happiness."

The young artist saw Lucas's face suddenly turn pale, and confusion stirred inside her. She stood rooted to the spot, unsure of what to do next.

Lucas stared at the pastor in astonishment, as if the whole world had suddenly become distant and unfamiliar. He simply couldn't comprehend why the pastor would say such things. To Lucas, this was never just a painting—it represented his faith in God, his longing for heaven, a sacred promise shared between him and Manon. It was the last spiritual pillar holding up his life.

With a trembling voice, Lucas asked the pastor, "Manon said she'd wait for me in heaven. Why is it I don't understand what you're saying?"

The pastor sighed deeply. "Lucas, heaven is the resting place for each of our souls. As long as you miss someone dearly, you will always meet them again—in your dreams."

With these words, the pastor sighed again, turned, and quietly walked away.

Chapter 4

At that moment, Lucas seemed barely able to stand. His entire body trembled, and his usually straight and dignified posture bent under the weight of his distress.

"Are you alright?" the girl asked gently, reaching out to help him sit down.

Lucas forced a faint smile, replying in a dry voice, "I'm fine. I'll be better after resting a moment."

They sat together quietly on a bench in the church garden. Lucas remained silent, his normally strong figure deflated, utterly drained of strength. It was only now apparent just how elderly he was.

The girl sat anxiously beside him, unsure what

had just happened.

The silence didn't last long. Lucas suddenly broke into uncontrollable sobs, tears streaming down his face.

Stunned by this sudden outburst, the girl felt panicked and helpless. She anxiously asked, "What's wrong, Lucas? What happened?"

Lucas's crying filled her heart with guilt and unease. She wasn't entirely sure what had occurred, but she knew it had to do with her dream. Deeply regretting mentioning it, she watched him helplessly weep, overwhelmed by self-blame.

After several deep breaths, Lucas gradually calmed himself. His voice trembled softly as he spoke, "Thirty-five years ago, I was stationed in Europe with the U.S. Army. During a vacation in Paris, I met the love of my life. Manon was like sunshine and fresh water to me—she made my life feel like heaven on earth.

"Seven years ago, when Manon's health was failing, she realized I intended to quietly follow her into death," Lucas continued softly. "She told me she'd never forgive me if I did that. Instead, she asked me to carry her blessing and bring happiness to everyone I met. She promised she would wait for me in heaven—her solemn promise.

"We were both devout Christians," Lucas continued. "Manon never lied once in her life—I believe in her with the same unwavering faith I have in God. She promised me that once I'd fulfilled my mission here, we would reunite in heaven and continue our happy life together forever.

"Manon asked me to bury her beside her parents. Every week, I visit her grave—not just because I fear she might forget me, but even more because I fear she might forget our promise. She never knew she had already taken my heart with her when she left."

As the young artist listened, tears quietly streamed down her face without her even noticing.

Lucas's voice shook even more. "God must exist—He certainly knows heaven is real. Manon is there, patiently waiting for me. She's waited seven years already, and I know I will find my way back to her."

Each of Lucas's words seemed to strike an invisible gate like a heavy hammer. The girl vividly saw Lucas reuniting with his beloved wife in heaven—a love transcending life and death itself, heartbreakingly beautiful.

Gently comforting Lucas, the girl said, "You're right. I believe there is always some force guiding us. Even if we can't directly feel His presence, no one can deny He exists."

As she spoke, the girl's eyes suddenly brightened with excitement. She jumped up and turned toward Lucas, saying, "I think I understand! Maybe that dream was meant to bring us together—to help us find answers together."

Lucas looked at her with confusion in his eyes.

The young artist continued enthusiastically, "Lucas, did you know? I've never shared this dream with anyone else. You're the first person I've told." Her voice brimmed with excitement, her whole being glowing with creative energy radiated like a sunlamp, illuminating everything around him.

Lucas was momentarily stunned by the girl's words. After a brief pause, he seemed to regain a thread of clarity before slowly raising his eyes to hers uncertainly. "You mean we should search for the answers together?"

The girl nodded firmly, "Of course—I want to know the answers, too."

"Why?" Lucas asked.

She looked at him curiously, "Why ask why? Artistic creation seeks resonance with the soul. Do we really need a reason to search for something that elevates our spirit?"

Lucas began to understand—true artists were indeed extraordinary people.

He then asked, "Do you believe in God?"

She hesitated briefly, then firmly nodded. "I do. Though I don't know exactly who He is or what He might be called, I believe He exists."

Lucas was slightly taken aback.

She gently explained, "There are many faiths in the world, each with its own God. I don't know if they're all manifestations of one deity or if only one is the true God. So, perhaps we should go to the Vatican and ask."

Lucas took a small notebook and pen from his pocket. While writing, he said aloud, "So, Question One: Does God exist, and who is He?"

"Bingo!" The young artist said excitedly.

Lucas continued thoughtfully, "Then Question Two: Where is God?"

The girl eagerly added, "And Question Three: What does He want us to do?"

Lucas smiled softly, shaking his head as he wrote down the third question. He was now certain this was God's arrangement. This girl had come from afar precisely to help him seek answers. The key to heaven's gates surely lay within these answers.

The girl excitedly suggested they travel to the Vatican to meet the Pope or an archbishop, admitting she'd never visited Italy before and had long dreamed of its artistic treasures, though she worried about not speaking Italian.

Lucas smiled warmly, understanding her better. "I once worked in Rome," he reassured her. "I speak Italian. You'll have no trouble with English in Rome—it's different from France."

Delighted, she eagerly asked, "Then, when shall we leave for Rome?"

Lucas was about to ask the girl about her itinerary in Paris, but seeing the exuberance in her expression, as if she might soar into the sky at any moment, he quickly changed his words: "I'll check flights and hotels now. Allow me to cover all expenses. I'm grateful you're willing to accompany an old man, and even more thankful you've set me on this journey to seek heaven."

The girl readily accepted his offer, warmly thanking him.

Chapter 5

Lucas and the young artist stood on a street near the Vatican, gazing toward St. Peter's Basilica towering gracefully in the distance. Its golden dome shimmered brilliantly under the sunlight, casting a divine glow as though touched by heaven itself. Set against the deep blue sky and drifting clouds, the basilica's silhouette exuded solemnity and grandeur. Immense stone columns and intricate carvings silently narrated a thousand years of history, every brick and stone whispering stories of faith and devotion.

Lucas drew in a deep breath, sensing the spiritual aura lingering in the air. An unexplainable tension stirred within him. He deeply hoped this sacred ground they were about to enter would hold the answers he sought.

Determination shone in Lucas's eyes as he straightened his posture and moved forward with steady, purposeful steps. The young artist followed closely behind, and together they slowly approached St. Peter's Basilica. As they drew nearer, the grandeur and solemnity of the cathedral became increasingly overwhelming, filling them both with awe.

The girl felt her heartbeat quicken, driven both by anticipation of the unknown and deep reverence for the faith embodied here. Turning slightly toward Lucas, she noticed that his face mirrored her own emotions—tension, expectation, and a subtle yet unmistakable sense of relief.

At last, they stepped through the cathedral's grand entrance. Instantly, all external noise faded into silence. Inside, the church was filled with a soft, mysterious glow, the air gently scented with a faint hint of incense, drawing them involuntarily into quiet reverence.

They walked slowly along the central aisle, each step as if tracing the veins of history, traversing a tunnel through time, into a sacred and solemn world. Sunlight gently filtered through colorful stained-glass windows, bathing the ancient sanctuary in a mysterious yet comforting glow.

Soon, their gaze settled upon a deeply moving sculpture—it depicted the Virgin Mary, head bowed gently in quiet contemplation. Her face bore profound sorrow, silently carrying the weight of all the world's suffering. Beneath her softly closed eyes lay boundless mourning, while her tender hands lovingly embraced the lifeless body of Jesus.

Jesus lay quietly in her arms, his expression peaceful, as though merely immersed in temporary sleep. There was no trace of pain—only serenity. Mary's flowing garments gently shifted with her movements, appearing almost to tremble softly in an invisible breeze. Although lifeless, Jesus's body radiated profound tranquility, as if his spirit had already ascended into heaven, leaving behind this earthly form for a mother's final, tender embrace.

Lucas stood motionless, captivated by the sculpture. His gaze shifted slowly between Mary and Jesus, a multitude of emotions stirring within him. In Mary, he recognized deep sorrow, powerlessness, unwavering yet helpless love, and profound attachment to her son. At the same time, in Jesus, he saw sacrifice and redemption—how willingly he had given his life to atone for humanity's sins, becoming an everlasting symbol of salvation.

Standing before the sculpture, the young artist felt deep reverence sweep through her. Tears filled her eyes as she experienced emotion too powerful for words.

"This is Michelangelo's *Pietà*," she murmured softly. "No matter how great our suffering or struggles, as long as we hold onto faith and hope, we'll always find peace and redemption within."

"I truly hope so," Lucas replied quietly before moving forward again.

Lucas and the young artist walked past rows of ancient pews until they reached a cabinet that appeared ordinary, yet emanated a mysterious aura. It was a confessional booth, decorated with inscriptions in languages from around the world—even Chinese among them. These engraved plaques stood like warm beacons, guiding every lonely soul seeking comfort and solace.

The girl waited quietly outside as Lucas took a deep breath and gently pushed open the door leading to a conversation of faith. Behind the door lay a small, peaceful space, with a soft cushion invitingly placed on the floor, ready to welcome every devout believer seeking solace in prayer.

Lucas slowly knelt, and as his knees touched the cushion, an unexpected comfort washed over him. Although a thin veil and mesh prevented him from clearly seeing the priest's face, the deep trust and longing from within his heart were strikingly clear.

Lucas quietly shared his story with the priest, speaking in English as he recounted his journey and the three questions carefully written in his notebook. The priest sat silently for a long while, offering no immediate response.

Just as Lucas began to wonder if the priest had fallen asleep, a warm, deep voice drifted softly through the thin veil: "My child, your experiences are indeed deeply moving. Yet remember, the path of faith is rarely smooth or easy. Many have come here with similar dreams and visions, seeking answers and yearning for truth. But true faith does not reside in external voices or illusions—it is found within, in the steadfast and luminous light of one's own heart."

Lucas lifted his head slightly, confusion evident in his voice. "Father, others have told me these dreams are merely reflections of my hopes, but there's a voice deep within me, insisting that God is guiding my path. I believe as long as faith resides in my heart, no matter how long or difficult the journey, I'll find the strength to keep moving forward."

The priest gently exhaled, his voice warm with understanding and encouragement. "My child, your courage and conviction are admirable. Faith is a deeply personal journey, needing neither validation nor judgment from the outside world. Hold firm to your beliefs, and each step you take will lead you closer to truth and illumination. May God's light always shine upon you, guiding your path forward."

Lucas seemed to grasp her meaning at first, but after a slight pause, he felt uncertainty creeping back in and gently asked once more, "Father, where exactly is God? Where is heaven? What does God want me to do?"

The priest took a deep breath, replying in his gentle, steady voice, "My child, within each of us lies a personal beacon of faith. At times, we question whether we truly hear God's voice or merely our soul whispering to us—expressions of internal struggles and desires, often mistaken for divine guidance."

Lucas's brow knitted with tension, uncertainty shifting into unease. He gazed intently at the gauzy curtain and asked in a low, resonant voice, "Father, have you ever heard the voice of God?"

The priest was momentarily taken aback, as if carefully weighing the meaning behind those words. After a thoughtful silence, he finally spoke, slowly and deliberately, "My child, every pure soul receives God's grace."

Lucas grew anxious, pressing urgently, "So—has God ever clearly told you what you should do?"

Sensing the conversation's end, the priest gently said, "My child, though I haven't heard God's voice myself, I've spent my life searching for Him. You told me you're searching as well—that's good. Perhaps it's best we each continue our search separately."

With those words, the priest closed the partition. Lucas heard him quietly leave. Lucas sank to the floor in regret, eyes unfocused, consumed by confusion.

After a long while, he slowly rose and stepped through the door. Not far away, the young artist sat in awe, her eyes sparkling with excitement and curiosity. Lucas smiled softly, feeling calmer.

Spotting Lucas, the girl hurried forward and asked eagerly, "How did it go? Did you find the answers?"

Lucas shook his head gently. "The priest said many things, but honestly, I didn't fully understand. I suppose I still need to keep searching."

Excitedly, the girl asked, "Then what's our next stop?"

Lucas smiled warmly. "My dear, we may have to travel to many places, speak with many people. You're young, with countless adventures ahead. Perhaps it's best we each continue these journeys on our own."

The young artist paused for a moment, then asked, "You mean we split up, each going our own way, and then I find ten more people to scatter in ten different directions?"

Lucas caught onto her joke and responded with a smile, "I'm not saying we should run away. My daughter has millions of followers. Maybe she could help—then we'd have a million paths! Who knows, it might be a good idea."

Chapter 6

At Rome Leonardo da Vinci International Airport, Lucas saw the young artist off as she boarded her flight back to Suzhou, China. Then, alone once more, he returned to Paris.

The autumn wind had begun to turn cold, sending fallen leaves dancing along the streets. Lucas drove his black private car toward Charles de Gaulle Airport, the peaceful smile he usually wore now replaced by a slight crease of worry between his brows.

Today's client was again traveling alone—an elderly Russian gentleman named Ivanov. "Who knows if that's even his real name," Lucas mused silently. "Seems every tough guy from Russia is called Ivanov."

After parking his car, Lucas picked up the sign bearing his client's name and walked into the arrivals hall.

He had just taken his place at the arrival gate, holding up the sign, when an elderly gentleman stepped confidently through the gate and approached him. Around seventy years old, the man had a stern yet dignified expression and a straight-backed bearing.

Two elderly gentlemen, each standing tall with dignity, shared a knowing smile as they simultaneously reached out their hands toward one another.

Old soldiers never die—they merely fade away. Two elderly men, connected by strikingly similar pasts, had silently acknowledged and accepted each other even before stepping into the car.

Lucas, a former U.S. Army soldier stationed in Europe and now a Christian struggling with his faith, carried a gaze that was both resolute and faintly sorrowful. Ivanov, a former Soviet veteran and equally perplexed member of the Russian Bolshevik Party, carried in his eyes stories tinged with melancholy and unfinished longing.

Lucas turned to his passenger, who had insisted on sitting beside him. "Ivan," he began softly, "the place we're headed—I visit every week. My beloved has been waiting there for me for seven years."

Ivanov nodded in understanding and glanced thoughtfully at Lucas. "I'm going to visit my comrade," he replied quietly. "For the sake of a dream we once shared, he's been resting silently there for over thirty years."

Lucas wasn't sure how to offer comfort. "We've both had people and causes worth sacrificing for," he said quietly. "Some people, some memories—they truly are unforgettable."

Ivanov looked at Lucas again, nodding solemnly. "You are a man I can trust."

Inside the car, the two elderly men, each immersed in their own thoughts, sat quietly, gazing straight ahead as the vehicle made its way toward the outskirts of Paris. Ivanov felt a surge of complex emotions rising within him. His mind drifted back to those passionate, turbulent years, as memories of each fallen comrade emerged vividly in his thoughts, one after another.

His purpose on this journey was clear—to visit all those comrades who now rested eternally in a foreign land. Ivanov knew deeply that this was not only his final visit, but also a profound spiritual cleansing and emotional homecoming.

They stepped out of the car together at the parking lot and quietly entered the cemetery. Aside from the soft chirping of birds and the rustling of autumn leaves stirred by the breeze, the vast graveyard was deeply tranquil.

Lucas and Ivanov stood silently, each before their separate gravestones, whispering quiet prayers in their hearts. Gentle sunlight filtered through melancholy clouds, casting mottled yet colorful patterns over their still-proud figures, etched by the passage of time.

At some point, Ivanov silently stood at attention and saluted the gravestone, his hand raised steadily, lingering in the air long after the moment had passed.

Recognizing this as a farewell salute, Lucas quietly stepped aside, respectfully waiting for the old soldier by the path.

After returning to the car, the sound of Lucas starting the engine gently filled the silence. Lucas finally broke the quiet, carefully asking, "Ivan, do you . . . still have something you believe in?"

Ivanov paused, momentarily caught off guard. The question touched something buried deep inside him. A trace of bitterness flickered through his eyes as he replied softly, "When we were young, who didn't have something to believe in? We would have given anything for our faith. In the mud and misery, we endured willingly. Even in despair, we faced death without hesitation. But now—I no longer know if their sacrifices meant anything." His voice broke, choked with emotion, and he fell silent.

Lucas reached out apologetically and patted Ivanov's shoulder. "Ivan, I'm so sorry—I didn't mean to upset you."

He then gently shared the promise he'd made with his wife, and the recent journey he'd undertaken to search for God and heaven, explaining what had motivated him to seek these answers.

Ivanov listened quietly and attentively. After Lucas finished, Ivanov looked at him thoughtfully and said, "Thank you for trusting me with your story. At our age, we all have ample time to reflect—to ponder where we came from, why we are here, and ultimately, where we are headed. These three great philosophical questions align closely with the central inquiries of religion. Ultimately, I believe everyone wants to know where their soul will rest in the end."

Lucas replied gratefully, "Although people have told me they've never seen God or heard His voice, I still firmly believe He exists. Somehow, beyond our understanding, two souls separated by oceans and continents can find lifelong love; strangers can instantly feel as if they've known each other forever; people with no connection at all can offer selfless help. And sometimes, inexplicably, individuals are willing to lay down their lives defending one another."

Lucas's voice grew increasingly passionate. "So, yes, I firmly believe there must be a higher power guiding us. The fact that I exist in this world at all—among countless possibilities—isn't because of my own doing. It's entirely by God's will. Would He abandon me? Perhaps, just as He has abandoned countless millions of failures, relinquishing those tainted souls. But conversely, I truly believe He would never forsake a pure, untainted soul."

Ivanov stared deeply into Lucas's eyes, a spark

slowly appearing in his gaze. With a hint of hesitation, he quietly asked, "Lucas, what do you think makes a soul corrupted?"

Lucas answered firmly, "Ivan, I'm not God—I can't provide an absolute answer. But I do know this: kindness represents purity, while evil symbolizes corruption. A kind soul will never intentionally harm others for personal gain, whereas an evil person will always cause harm if it serves their own interests."

Ivanov pressed further, "But what if harm arises from conflicts in belief, like the situation between your people and mine, thirty years ago?"

Lucas smiled gently, speaking sincerely. "Ivan, unless placed in a scenario where only one side could walk away alive, we would never have fought to the death. Neither of us ever intended to hurt the other's family. We were human beings then, just as we are now, with our humanity, conscience, and moral boundaries still intact. That's why, ultimately, we were—and remain—good people."

Lucas took a deep breath, then spoke in a low, reflective voice. "Ivan, both of us have walked to the very edge of the abyss. You know as well as I do—those who dance with demons are most vulnerable to temptation. But, fortunately, neither of us ever gave in. We held onto our conscience and kindness. We stayed true to those we loved."

Ivanov had never imagined that his life could receive such affirmation. Grateful and moved, his voice took on a dreamy quality: "Lucas, oh Lucas, I genuinely appreciate your affirmation. I completely agree with you. Now, I too want to know—who is He, and where is heaven?"

Lucas responded with enthusiasm, "Ivan, let's each search for the answers. A young woman from the East once jokingly suggested finding ten people and splitting into ten separate paths. I told her, perhaps we could find a million people, each taking a unique path. I truly believe that if we keep looking, we'll find what we seek."

Ivanov smiled, visibly relieved and at peace. "Yes, Lucas—I believe it too. I have no family remaining, but I had comrades who stood by my side through life and death. They were my brothers, my true family. When the time comes, I want to reach heaven—and, even more importantly, I want to bring them along with me, to a place of eternal peace and happiness."

Chapter 7

Ivanov departed for Germany, determined to visit all his comrades who rested forever in foreign lands. Smiling warmly, he told Lucas he would find one hundred people, each taking their separate paths, tirelessly searching for answers.

The wind in Paris had grown colder, and the leaves once scattered across the streets had vanished to unknown corners. Lucas drove his black sedan to the airport once again. Today's guests were a family of four from Jordan.

At Charles de Gaulle Airport, Lucas welcomed the family of Fadi Abdullah. Fadi and his lovely wife traveled with their two children—their ten-year-old son, Amin, and their eight-year-old daughter, Iman. Both children were well-mannered, their gentle and charming personalities blending perfectly together.

Fadi's family planned to spend four days exploring Paris, visiting its famous historical landmarks as well as renowned cultural and artistic sites. The two children brimmed with curiosity about this iconic city of medieval and Renaissance heritage. As they traveled through the streets, Amin and Iman whispered softly to each other, their faces glowing with excitement and delight at the sights passing by.

Over the following days, Lucas served as guide, interpreter, and driver for Fadi's family. Throughout their delightful journey, Fadi occasionally asked thoughtful questions, but it was the endless creativity and imaginative questions from the two children that truly brightened each day. Fadi's wife observed her husband and children lovingly, a gentle smile never leaving her face. At their enthusiastic request,

Lucas proudly introduced them daily to the rich culinary culture of France.

Lucas found himself genuinely intrigued by Fadi's family—their lifestyle, customs, and cultural background. Though he'd previously interacted with guests from the Middle East, this was the first time he'd experienced such warm and open-hearted communication. Amin and Iman, too, eagerly showed great interest in both American and French cultures. Their mutual curiosity and joyful exchanges about each other's cultures filled their days with continuous laughter and lively conversation.

Soon, it was the family's final day exploring Paris. Lucas would drive them to the airport tomorrow morning. When they returned to the hotel in the early evening, Fadi warmly invited Lucas to join them for dinner. Lucas gratefully accepted the invitation. The leisurely pace of a traditional French dinner provided the perfect opportunity for friends to enjoy conversation together.

Lucas asked gently, "Fadi, it seems like most Arabs around the world practice Islam. In your teachings, is there a description of heaven? If so, how does your religion describe it?"

Fadi laughed heartily, his voice warm and cheerful. "Lucas, Arabs are not the only ones who worship Allah—there are countless believers around the globe who offer Him praise." Gazing upward through the window with eyes full of longing, he continued softly, "Almighty Allah gathers every pure soul back into His embrace. That's where our heaven lies."

Lucas watched him quietly, feeling deeply moved. It struck him profoundly that the heaven Fadi described, just like Ivanov's depiction from the Eastern Orthodox tradition, bore an extraordinary resemblance to the heavens described by both Protestant and Catholic teachings.

Fadi continued patiently and passionately, sharing with Lucas the beauty of his faith. He explained Islam's Five Pillars and described how believers practice their religion in everyday life. He spoke of the reverence Muslims have for Allah, their yearning for the afterlife, and the fundamental teachings of honesty, justice, generosity, and respect for life and nature. He also touched on dietary restrictions, the timing of daily prayers, and the rituals associated with them.

As Lucas listened, his expression grew increasingly solemn. Looking thoughtfully at Fadi, he said, "Your devotion to your faith is truly inspiring; your steadfastness and passion deeply move me."

Turning to Fadi with sincere gratitude, Lucas continued, "Thank you, Fadi. I think I'm beginning to understand. Tell me if this sounds right: Regardless of one's specific faith, belief is what prevents us from becoming lost along life's journey. Religion, or faith itself, gives us direction—and as long as we follow that path faithfully, we'll surely find our way to heaven."

Fadi placed his hand gently over his heart and bowed slightly. "It's my honor to have been of help," he replied warmly. A bittersweet smile appeared on his face as he continued, "It puzzles me sometimes—in America and Europe, there are always people who struggle to understand or accept our faith. In truth, we're simply following our hearts, quietly walking a peaceful path toward our own paradise of happiness. Why do some feel the need to impose their beliefs on us? If I can respect their faith and understand their choices, why can't they offer us the same in return?"

Lucas nodded repeatedly in agreement. "Someday, people will come to realize that despite our differing beliefs, kindness and sincerity among human hearts can transcend boundaries. When that moment arrives, the barriers dividing faiths will melt away, leaving only our shared longing for life's beauty and the purity of our souls."

Fadi was slightly puzzled by Lucas's sudden intensity. With gentle concern, he asked, "Lucas, I'm very grateful for your understanding, but you seem a little emotional—are you alright?"

Realizing his voice had risen more than intended, Lucas quickly lowered his tone and offered a quiet apology, nodding politely towards Fadi and the curious diners nearby. Seeing Fadi's confused expression, Lucas softly explained the promise he'd made with his wife and the deep questions he had been wrestling with ever since.

A soft, suppressed sobbing drew their attention—Fadi's wife, quiet through much of their visit, was gently weeping, visibly touched by Lucas's heartfelt revelation. With sincerity and heartfelt warmth, she said, "Lucas, you will surely find your way to heaven. You will reunite with your beloved, and together you'll live happily in heaven. May Almighty Allah bless you!"

Lucas felt momentarily startled—Allah's blessing? Yet he quickly understood the sincerity behind her words and thanked her graciously for her kind wishes. Sorrow would eventually fade. Although their beliefs differed, they shared the same kindness in their hearts and nobility of soul.

Under the glow of streetlights in Paris, people everywhere gave thanks to their own Gods and enjoyed their dinners in countless unique ways. The night breeze was chilly, yet it couldn't diminish the warmth radiating from each home, filling the city with humanity and love.

Lucas didn't mention the joke about finding a thousand people to scatter in a thousand directions to Fadi. Although Fadi was easygoing by nature, Lucas knew that Fadi's faith was something never to be joked about.

The following morning, Lucas drove Fadi and his family to the airport, the sunlight gently lingering upon them, as if reluctant to let them go. When Fadi warmly invited Lucas to visit Jordan, Lucas graciously accepted the offer and embraced Fadi affectionately. Yet deep within, Lucas knew this was their final embrace in this lifetime—any future reunion would only occur in heaven.

Chapter 8

Winter had finally arrived in Paris. Lucas once again left the cemetery, driving his black sedan through the bustling city streets.

Today, he was headed again to Charles de Gaulle Airport, this time to welcome two young women from Canada.

Sophia and Ivy, both energetic and youthful, sat in the back seat. They had come to Paris to attend an event organized by an international environmental organization.

From the moment they stepped into the car, the two girls exchanged warm gestures and playful laughter. Their vibrant spirit filled the space like rays of winter sunlight streaming through the windows, warming Lucas's heart and brightening the atmosphere.

A knowing glint appeared in Lucas's eyes, and a faint smile crept across his face unconsciously.

Sophia explained that they would attend a two-day environmental summit starting the day after tomorrow. They had arrived a day early, partly to adjust to the time difference, but more importantly, to fulfill their dream of visiting the Louvre Museum.

With excitement, Ivy said, "The treasures inside the Louvre are sparkling jewels of human civilization. Protecting all the beautiful things in this world is our lifelong mission."

Her words were sincere and heartfelt. Sophia gently embraced Ivy, silently agreeing.

In the rearview mirror, Lucas's smile deepened—not just with warmth, but also with genuine respect.

Turning to the two girls, Lucas asked politely, "If you don't mind me asking, could you tell me more about your summit?"

Ivy beamed with pride. "Of course we don't mind! We're attending an international youth summit for environmental delegates from around the world. During the event, our angel Sophia will deliver a remarkable speech."

"Really? That's wonderful!" Lucas said with delight. "Would I be lucky enough to attend and hear it in person?"

Sophia playfully nudged Ivy and replied warmly, "Mr. Lucas, it would be my honor to have you in the audience for my speech."

Two mornings later, the three parked near the convention center. Lucas followed Sophia and Ivy into the main auditorium. The hall, capable of seating nearly two thousand, was already filled with a thousand attendees, with more guests steadily arriving.

Sophia went backstage to prepare. Lucas and Ivy sat near the front. Glancing at the event schedule, Lucas saw Sophia was listed as the third speaker. Her talk was titled: "Heaven or Hell."

Upon seeing the title, Lucas's eyes narrowed slightly. He lifted his gaze thoughtfully toward the auditorium's vaulted ceiling. Beyond the stage lights, countless stars silently shimmered in the unseen cosmos. Could it be, he wondered, that every encounter, every step, was part of God's purpose?

Amid warm applause, Sophia stepped onto the stage. Her simple makeup did nothing to dull the radiance of her youthful energy. Her gentle yet powerful voice filled the hall as she began her speech.

"Honorable members of the organizing committee, distinguished guests, and all those devoted to environmental protection—greetings to you all!

"Today, I'm truly honored to be invited here. My speech is titled 'Heaven or Hell,' based on reflections from my eight years of environmental advocacy, sharing it here with everyone.

"Stanford neuroscientist David Eagleman once proposed an intriguing idea. He said humans experience three types of death: biological death, when the body ceases to function; social death, when one loses legal identity and recognition in society; and spiritual death—when one's presence and influence vanish completely.

"The first two forms are fairly straightforward. However, spiritual death occurs when a person's character and unique spark disappear entirely from the world. No one remembers them, leaving no trace, as if they never existed. This final form of death would signify the complete disappearance of one's spiritual existence from the world.

"At nine years old, an accidental viewing of a horror scene made me deeply afraid of death. For weeks, I struggled to sleep, often waking from nightmares. My parents began taking me to church every Sunday, gradually calming my heart.

"One Sunday after service, my father took me to the church cemetery, where we placed flowers on the grave of our elderly neighbor, Mrs. Connie. On the way home, my father told me, 'Each of us will reach life's end someday. Death isn't frightening; what's truly frightening is a soul with nowhere to go. God gave us the dignity of being human, stewards of this planet. If we live only like animals—eating, sleeping, and merely existing—how are we honoring His grace?'

"My father once said, 'Our lifetime is just a fleeting moment in this vast universe. Many pursuits people chase may ultimately be meaningless. So remember, sweetheart, if you can do even one thing truly beneficial to humanity or the world, when you reach life's end, you can proudly offer that deed back to God. That one meaningful act will be your soul's passport back to His embrace.'

"I'm deeply grateful to my father. From that day forward, I eagerly sought opportunities to help others—once even volunteering to take my neighbor's child to the park, only to find myself surrounded by police officers there."

The audience burst into warm laughter.

"At last, I discovered a cause genuinely meaningful to humanity and our planet. What could be more crucial to human civilization than environmental protection?"

The auditorium erupted in thunderous applause.

"A poet from the distant East once wrote: 'Some people are alive, but in the hearts of others, they are already dead. Some have died, yet live forever in others' hearts.'

"In reality, we often encounter people who, for personal gain, sacrifice society's greater good. Aside from their allies, everyone else likely wishes they'd simply disappear."

Another wave of applause filled the hall.

"Conversely, those who quietly devote themselves and even sacrifice their lives for humanity's welfare are true heroes, forever alive in our hearts."

Resounding applause again swept through the auditorium.

"Each of us holds only modest power to change

the world. We might spend a lifetime making slight improvements—or perhaps seeing no visible change at all. Yet without our collective efforts, what would the world become?"

The applause returned, loud and unwavering.

"This world can become our heaven—or descend into a hell for future generations. Right now, we must use whatever strength we possess to persuade others to join us. Together, we can transform this world. Even if we find ourselves in hell, we'll work tirelessly to create heaven on Earth!"

The applause surged skyward. Everyone in the audience rose, giving Sophia a standing ovation. Sophia bowed graciously, but the applause seemed endless.

Lucas stood up, clapping with deep emotion. The young woman on stage radiated brilliance. He felt deeply grateful for hearing this speech, profoundly touched by Sophia's inspiring words.

Two days later, on the way to the airport, Ivy

playfully teased from the back seat, "Lucas, are you going to discriminate against us?"

Lucas looked puzzled. "Why would I?"

Ivy grinned. "I knew you wouldn't. We're more than just partners in the same cause—we're soulmates."

Lucas smiled warmly. "You haven't hurt anyone. Your souls are purer and nobler than most I've known. I'm honored to have met you on this life journey."

The two girls responded in perfect harmony, "So are we!"

Their laughter filled the car, wrapping the moment in warmth and joy.

Chapter 9

It was a bright, sunny day in Paris. Though the breeze along the banks of the River Seine still carried a hint of winter's chill, fresh green buds had begun to emerge from bare branches—spring was quietly arriving in the city.

In a parking lot near the docks of the Seine, Lucas greeted his newest passenger: a cheerful British woman in her eighties. Her silver-white hair gleamed gently in the sunlight, complementing the elegant pearl necklace and soft pastel scarf draped gracefully around her shoulders. Her eyes sparkled with a gaze as pure as a child's, and every smile she shared seemed to fill the car with warmth, radiating youthful vitality, despite her age.

Lucas respectfully welcomed Mrs. Smith into the car.

"Oh, Lucas, no need to be so formal," she replied brightly, her voice full of a delightful London lilt. "You're not exactly a youngster yourself—you could call me Annie."

She quickly proved herself an engaging conversationalist. "Did you know, Lucas? I've been traveling continuously for three years now. I embarked on a cruise around the world, and for the past two months, I've been leisurely exploring the towns along the Seine. France is the final stop on this grand adventure of mine." Annie explained cheerfully that she intended to revisit her favorite spots in Paris—the charming cafés near Montmartre, the gardens at Versailles, and perhaps even enjoy a leisurely evening cruise along the Seine.

Lucas was genuinely surprised. "Have you been traveling alone all this time?"

Annie smiled, clearly delighted by his astonishment. "Absolutely! When I turned sixty, my husband John was ecstatic—finally, he said, we could properly enjoy our retirement. He told me, 'Annie, we're still young enough. While we can still walk and eat, why don't we go see the world?' And so, John and I set out together. That was my first journey around the globe."

As she spoke, Annie's voice softened slightly. But soon enough, she smiled again and continued cheerfully, "When I turned seventy, I told myself, 'Annie, you're still not too old. While you can still walk, while you can still enjoy your food, why don't you travel around the world again?' So, that's when I began my first solo trip around the globe."

Lucas listened quietly, sensing it was best not to ask further about her personal situation.

Annie went on happily, "Then, three years ago, at eighty, I said to myself again, 'Annie, you might finally be getting old—but you can still walk, you can still eat—so why not travel the world one more time?' And now, here I am. This is my third trip around the world."

Lucas couldn't help but express his admiration. "Annie, you're truly remarkable. I've thought countless times about traveling around the world, but I've never managed to do it. Now it feels less and less likely."

Annie noticed a faint sadness in his eyes. She offered gently, "Lucas, compared to me, you're still young. You seem to be in very good health. While you still have your strength—while you can still walk and eat—you should see this beautiful world. Don't let yourself have regrets."

Lucas gave a slightly bitter smile, but said nothing.

Annie sighed softly. "John was a doctor, fourteen years older than me. Throughout his life, he was always waiting for me. He first saw me when I was fourteen years old, and he quietly waited as I grew up. It wasn't until I was twenty-four that I finally fell in love with him—by then, he was already thirty-eight. Before retiring, I worked as a lawyer. I loved helping people in need, and I truly enjoyed my work. John retired at sixty-five. He loved to travel, and his dream was to see the world. But instead, he patiently waited at home for another nine years, until my sixtieth birthday, when I suddenly realized he'd grown old, and that now it was my turn to accompany him."

At this point, Annie glanced at Lucas, took a deep breath, and said gently, "Lucas, some things in life, once missed, can never be found again."

Lucas looked slightly dazed.

Annie felt she needed to offer a bit more persuasion. "You know, I never actually liked traveling when I was younger. I preferred staying quietly at home, reading a good book. But when I went traveling around the world with John and saw the joy on his face, how he laughed and smiled like a child, I suddenly fell in love with traveling. John left me when he was eighty-two. Two years after he passed away, I felt as if John wanted to invite me on another trip. So, I took his photo along and retraced the same route we had traveled together."

She pulled out a necklace, opened a small heart-shaped locket, and showed Lucas a picture of herself with John. Their smiles radiated happiness, as warm and bright as the spring sunshine.

Annie's face lit up once again with a childlike, innocent smile. "Three years ago, I worried that soon I might not be able to travel anymore, so once again, I brought John's photo and retraced our footsteps once more."

Only then did Lucas realize that the words Annie had spoken to herself before the second and third journeys were actually the very same words her husband had said to her on her sixtieth birthday. Without realizing it, tears began to stream down Lucas's face. Deep longing was always so quietly simple, and true love was always so humble.

Seeing his tears, Annie looked apologetic and opened her mouth to speak.

Lucas offered Annie a reassuring gesture. With a bittersweet smile, he softly explained, "My wife passed away seven years ago. She promised me we'd reunite in heaven someday. She rests in this city, and every week I go to visit her, afraid she might forget me. So, you see, I can't leave this city for too long."

Annie gently patted Lucas's arm without saying a word. Now she understood why she had revealed so much about her past to Lucas—they were both people bound by love. Neither of them ever intended to free themselves from those bonds, because both were patiently waiting for the day that special person would welcome them again.

After a long silence, Annie asked softly, "Lucas, as a former lawyer, it's hard to call myself a truly devout Christian. So, tell me—do you think heaven really exists?"

"Of course it does," Lucas answered earnestly.

His voice was gentle yet resolute, conveying an unwavering conviction. "I believe in the existence of the Lord. I believe every pure soul returns to His embrace. There's only love and goodness there, and the people we cherish are there, waiting patiently for us. Our faith is the bridge we cross to reach heaven."

As Annie listened, her eyes reflected a gentle glow—as though she, too, could glimpse the heaven where John was waiting for her.

"Oh, Lucas, that's truly wonderful," she said warmly. "I believe you. I'm sure John is already there, waiting patiently for me again. My dear, patient John . . . he's been waiting fifteen years already. Poor man, he might have to wait another fifteen."

And then Annie began laughing brightly, joyfully, just like a child.

Chapter 10

The spring breeze always had a way of soothing the ache of farewells. Along the banks of the Seine, fresh green buds seemed to embody silent thoughts of longing. By the lake, a little girl about five or six years old toddled along, imitating the waddle of two ducks. Her mother stood nearby, snapping pictures with her phone, capturing these precious moments.

Lucas observed the American mother and daughter from a distance. He guessed they were here to relax and clear their minds, as their itinerary over the past few days had mostly involved leisurely strolls through various royal gardens. He understood—

children at such a young age rarely found much appeal in the Louvre's art galleries.

During their travels, Lucas served as their quiet, considerate companion, always close by to help whenever needed. The mother's name was Alice; her daughter was Flora. Flora, a delicate child with soft, wavy hair, had an innocence that seemed to mask an underlying sadness. Alice's golden hair cascaded gently over her shoulders, her expressive eyes often shadowed with unspoken melancholy. Though Lucas couldn't put his finger on why, he sensed a forced brightness in Flora's innocent smiles, as if she was trying to please someone. Likewise, Alice's laughter often concealed subtle sadness or regret.

Lucas refrained from prying into their personal matters. Instead, in the journey that followed, he did his best to keep Flora entertained—playing hide-and-seek, skipping stones across the water, and making flower crowns together—to help the little girl forget whatever weighed on her mind. He loved hearing children laugh without a care. It reminded him of when his own daughter, Georgia, had been young. Whenever she seemed troubled, he would distract her with playful games until she forgot all her worries.

On their last evening together, Alice invited Lucas to join them for dinner at the hotel restaurant downstairs. Lucas graciously accepted. After dinner, Flora, exhausted from several days of play, appeared ready for bed. Alice turned to Lucas and asked sincerely, "Would you mind waiting a bit? Maybe we could have a drink afterward?"

Lucas simply nodded, indicating his agreement. Alice took Flora upstairs to their room to put the little girl to sleep before returning.

Paris's streetlights painted the night with shimmering colors, their glow illuminating Alice's golden hair at the window seat, adding touches of neon brilliance. Alice ordered a whiskey, swirling the amber liquid thoughtfully, while Lucas opted for a mojito, savoring its refreshing mint aroma. With gentle music playing softly in the background, he quietly listened as Alice began her story.

Alice smiled softly, though a trace of sorrow lingered in her expression as she began, "Lucas, I really can't thank you enough for everything you've done for Flora these past few days."

She raised her hand, gently interrupting Lucas's modesty. "You've been like an angel sent by God, bringing warmth to both of us."

Alice lifted her glass, cutting off Lucas's polite protests, and continued, "Shortly before we came to Paris, Jerry and I divorced. We both feel incredibly guilty about Flora. When she was born, we promised each other she'd grow up happy, like a little princess . . ."

Lucas raised his glass and gently clinked it against Alice's, offering quiet comfort.

Alice took a small sip before continuing softly, "Flora is extremely sensitive. She can't understand why her father doesn't want her in his life anymore.

Every day, she worries that her mother might suddenly decide not to want her either. Because she said the day before her dad left, he was holding her hand, walking and laughing with her. He carried her home in his arms, promising that he'd always love her. So now she wonders if it was something she did wrong. Every day, she keeps promising me she'll listen, she'll behave, she'll never throw another tantrum . . ."

Alice's voice caught, tears choking her words. Lucas quietly handed her a napkin.

Alice drained her glass in one go and continued quietly, "I'm an elementary school teacher, but I don't know how to tell my daughter that none of this is her fault—or even Jerry's. Because her father is truly a remarkable man. The problem is, his greatness belongs to the whole world, but Flora and I simply needed him to belong to us."

Lucas was intrigued. "Would you tell me about Flora's father?"

Alice motioned to the waiter for another drink.

"Jerry was a stock analyst, an Ivy League graduate. Eight years ago, he walked away from his career on Wall Street and moved to California. He took every penny he had earned and established a nonprofit charity. I was his first employee—and his first admirer. Fresh out of college, I fell recklessly in love with him.

"Together we traveled to Africa, the Middle East, South Asia, Latin America—delivering food, medicine, clothes, and water purification devices to people who desperately needed them. We faced war zones, diseases, accidents, poisonous insects, and dangerous animals. But no matter what peril confronted us, we always faced it bravely—together."

"What made you so brave? Was it your faith?" Lucas couldn't help asking.

Alice paused, startled. "Jerry is an atheist—but he's not a communist either. I guess . . . it was love."

Seeing Lucas's puzzled expression, she quickly explained, "Jerry left Wall Street because he believed capitalism would endlessly take and exploit. Beneath the dazzling surface of wealth and success, he saw a body that reeked of decay. America's middle class shrank from sixty percent to forty percent, and the wealthy class from twenty percent to just ten percent. Millions upon millions—thirty percent of our population—were slipping backward, their quality of life steadily eroding. And outside the United States, millions lived decade after decade, barely achieving basic survival. Jerry always wondered: if God truly exists, how could He allow all this suffering?

"Jerry always said his conscience wouldn't allow him to look away. He knew one person's strength was limited, but he had to do what he felt was right," Alice continued gently. "He always told me if the world ever lost all love, everyone would live in hell. But as long as even a shred of love remains, our world still has a chance at redemption. And when our world finally becomes filled with love and warmth, it will become heaven itself."

Listening intently, Lucas felt a deep sense of respect. His mind flashed back to Sofia, the young environmentalist, standing confidently on the stage. Sofia and Jerry were both remarkable people. Both possessed noble, pure souls. It was people like them who ensured the world still basked in rays of hope. They might not worship a traditional God, but they unquestionably lived lives defined by profound faith. In the eyes of those they served, these selfless heroes were gods themselves, lighting their own lives on fire to illuminate and warm the lives of others.

With admiration and a touch of bitterness in her voice, Alice continued, "Jerry's radiant humanity deeply captivated me. After overcoming countless hardships together, he proposed, and we got married. We had a child together, and to better care for her, I obtained my teaching certificate and became an elementary school teacher."

Alice's voice became quieter. "Jerry continued

pursuing his dreams, traveling through jungles and distant villages around the globe. Every time he left home, I worried endlessly about the dangers he might face. His heart carried the weight of the entire world, but mine carried only him. Eventually, our views diverged, our relationship strained. I grew exhausted and asked for a divorce. I would have given Jerry everything, but I had to take care of Flora. Jerry left, leaving the house behind for us, but my heart feels empty."

Lucas finished his drink thoughtfully and sighed gently. "Alice, it's clear you still love him. Jerry talked about how the world needs that last shred of love—but isn't the same true for your own family? If the love between you disappears completely, your home would feel like a living hell. But when you fill your home with love and warmth, it becomes your own little heaven."

Lucas paused, suddenly struck by his own words. A new understanding dawned upon him. He glanced up to see Alice staring back in astonishment, and he realized she had understood, too.

Smiling warmly, Lucas added, "I truly hope you, Jerry, and Flora find your way back to your personal heaven. Perhaps you should adopt a cat named Tom—Jerry might hurry back, since Tom and Jerry always seem happiest when they're chasing each other."

Alice burst into laughter, spontaneous and genuine, as if long-awaited sunlight had finally broken through into her heart, bright and clear once more.

Chapter 11

It was another bright, sunny morning, with a gentle spring breeze lifting smiles onto people's faces. Today, Lucas was scheduled to pick up a Japanese couple, Mr. Yamamoto and his wife.

At the arrivals hall of Charles de Gaulle Airport in Paris, Lucas met his two guests. Mr. Yamamoto appeared to be in his sixties, short in stature but impeccably dressed, exuding a calm and confident smile. His eyes radiated quiet intelligence, and his neatly combed white hair conveyed a dignified sophistication accumulated over time. Mrs. Yamamoto was elegantly dressed, her refined attire enhancing her graceful beauty. She wore an elegant silk kimono decorated with subtle floral patterns, the obi sash neatly tied at her waist, accentuating her poised elegance. Her hair was carefully styled, adorned with a delicate kanzashi hairpin, and she carried a small embroidered handbag. She moved delicately yet effortlessly, perfectly matching her husband's rhythm.

The Yamamotos bowed respectfully. "Mr. Lucas, my name is Kyojiro Yamamoto. We apologize for any inconvenience and appreciate your assistance."

Lucas found himself momentarily at a loss due to the traditional Japanese greeting. Given his tall frame, he feared that if he bowed similarly, their heads might awkwardly collide. He hesitated, unsure whether to offer a handshake or support them, making the moment even more awkward.

His confusion prompted Mrs. Yamamoto to cover her mouth and laugh gently. Mr. Yamamoto joined in with an understanding smile. "My apologies, Mr. Lucas. It was I who was rude." His voice carried a warmth that blended softly with the morning breeze.

The hotel where the Yamamotos stayed was luxurious, and their itinerary had been meticulously arranged by Mr. Yamamoto's assistant, who had coordinated everything with Lucas beforehand. Lucas had initially worried about potential communication barriers, but was relieved to discover that Mr. Yamamoto spoke excellent English.

Over the next two days, Mr. and Mrs. Yamamoto showed an extraordinary interest in Renaissance art, treasures, and monuments. Lucas, however, never anticipated that someone would genuinely inquire about the price of a Monet painting. After repeatedly apologizing for his inability to provide such information, Lucas was relieved when Mr. Yamamoto seemed to realize his question might have been unintentionally inappropriate.

Surprisingly, Mrs. Yamamoto, who had only spoken Japanese with her husband thus far, suddenly revealed her excellent English skills. "Mr. Lucas," she gently asked, "would you mind telling us a bit about European religions and sacred places? I'm very curious about them."

Lucas happily obliged, enthusiastically talking about the Virgin Mary and Jesus Christ, and concluding by mentioning a church event taking place that day. The Yamamotos listened attentively.

"Would you like to attend this church event?" Lucas warmly invited them.

Mr. Yamamoto smiled and politely shook his head. "Thank you very much, Lucas. When traveling through Europe, understanding its religious culture is essential to truly appreciating its history and people. It's sufficient for us to learn about it and visit some famous historical sites. Attending church activities might not be appropriate, as my wife and I practice Buddhism."

Intrigued, Lucas invited the Yamamotos to rest at a nearby café. Once seated, he asked curiously,

"Mr. Yamamoto, would you mind telling me a little about Japanese Buddhism? I'm very interested."

Yamamoto gazed dreamily toward the east, his eyes distant yet tender. "When I was a child, my father gently took my hand as we climbed ancient stone-paved stairs leading up to a hillside temple said to be over three hundred years old. Each time, my father would first cleanse us with water from the stone basin, make an offering of incense money, and then strike the large bronze temple bell, its deep resonant chime echoing gently through the serene mountain air. Those moments remain my most cherished memories, for I later discovered my father had always been quietly praying for my happiness."

Yamamoto's voice grew softer. "Eventually, my father's legs grew frail, each step becoming too great a struggle for him to climb to the temple he so loved. I began going alone, repeating the rituals my father had taught me, but now my prayers were for him. Later, when I became a father myself, I took my son's hand and guided him up those same stone steps. Now, my own legs are beginning to fail, yet I still climb to that ancient temple at least once a month. To me, that place is my spiritual sanctuary." Mr. Yamamoto smiled gently, his voice echoing softly, like the distant ringing of a mountain bell. The sound resonated with a serene, lingering harmony.

Lucas nodded slowly. "Your words feel like the sound of distant temple bells."

"I'm enchanted by that soothing bell," Yamamoto continued quietly. "It purifies my soul. Whenever I hear its ethereal sound, I forget the distractions of this world and immerse myself in extraordinary calmness."

He sighed softly. "I've spent my life as a businessman, a profession often burdened with material pursuits and relentless pressures, which is why I feel I need spiritual cleansing more than most."

Lucas was momentarily caught off guard by this sudden shift in conversation, and Mr. Yamamoto offered no further explanation.

Lucas decided to ask directly, "Mr. Yamamoto, does your religion describe heaven?"

Mr. Yamamoto smiled gently. "In Buddhism, heaven is called the 'Pure Land.' The beings you call God, we call Buddhas; your angels, we call Bodhisattvas. Life itself is described as a sea of suffering because it traps impure souls in cycles of despair. The Pure Land lies beyond this sea, and both Buddhas and Bodhisattvas compassionately reach out to guide those lost in suffering, an act we call 'universal salvation.'"

Yamamoto sighed softly, adding, "As a businessman, I've spent half my life pursuing profit. Now, I no longer wish to drown in greed and desire. Instead, I long for inner peace and tranquility. I'm waiting for redemption, hoping someday a Bodhisattva will lead me to the Pure Land."

Yamamoto's voice grew increasingly calm and serene, as simple and unpretentious as when he had casually asked about the price of Monet's paintings a few days earlier.

Lucas realized that, despite the differences in Eastern and Western cultures or beliefs, what everyone ultimately seeks on life's journey is inner peace and tranquility. Could this, perhaps, be the true essence of happiness? Could it truly be this simple? After all, every accomplished and renowned person in the world, upon growing old, takes pride in having reached precisely this state. Lucas mused that those still chasing dreams or just starting their journeys might not realize the wounds they endured and the strength they expended were merely reflections of their own desires. Ultimately, they might earn only a bitter smile, or worse—a quiet sigh from someone else.

Lucas silently prayed for Mr. Yamamoto, wishing him steadfastness in his quest for tranquility. Perhaps someday, a Bodhisattva truly would guide him safely to the other shore.

After dropping Mr. and Mrs. Yamamoto off at the airport, Lucas once again drove to visit Manon. Standing before his wife's gravestone, he spoke animatedly, sharing stories about the people he'd met and his evolving understanding of heaven. Lucas reassured Manon, promising he would eventually find the answer he sought.

As he emerged from the cemetery along the shaded avenue, the spring sunshine was warm and gentle, as comforting as Manon's own touch. Suddenly, the radiant light seemed to illuminate everything, blending seamlessly with him, enveloping him entirely.

Chapter 12

In the instant Lucas lost consciousness, time seemed to freeze. Lucas didn't know how long he'd been asleep; everything around him had become blurry and distant, until a gentle voice softly called to him, drawing him back from his dreams.

Slowly, Lucas opened his eyes, finding himself in a place both familiar and strangely distant.

"Hmm? Is this a hospital room? Why is everything in English?"

"Dad, you're awake!" a tearful voice exclaimed beside him. It was his daughter, Georgia, her face filled with concern and relief. She tightly gripped his hand, exhaustion and sadness clearly etched on her features.

Lucas glanced around slowly, realizing he was indeed in a hospital. Evidently, his body had finally given out.

"Which hospital is this?" Lucas's voice came out weak and raspy, barely above a whisper.

"Dad, we're in a hospital in Seattle, Washington. I brought you back from the hospital in Paris," Georgia whispered softly, her voice breaking as tears welled up again. "How could you hide your illness from me? How could you keep me in the dark—how could you bear to do this to me? I've already lost Mom. I can't bear to lose you, too! Do you both not want me anymore?"

Georgia's voice cracked, and she collapsed into Lucas's embrace, sobbing uncontrollably.

At that moment, the hospital door opened quietly. A nurse stepped inside, gently but firmly shushing Georgia. "Ma'am, please, you need to calm down. I understand how you feel, but we must keep the patient from getting agitated. Staying calm will greatly aid his recovery."

After apologizing together to the nurse, Lucas softly stroked Georgia's hair. "I'm sorry, sweetheart, truly sorry. Georgia, I just didn't want you to worry. Your mom and I always hoped you'd live every day happily."

"No!" Georgia interrupted through her tears. "Mom's gone, and I'm not happy. You can't leave me, Dad—I need you here. I'll go get married right now if that's what it takes. You have to be at my wedding, attend your grandchild's baptism, you have to . . ."

Lucas raised a trembling hand to gently wipe away her endless tears. "Sweetheart, please forgive me. Believe me, I truly wish I could do those things. But your mother has been waiting for me in heaven for almost eight years. Every single day, my heart aches for her. Forgive me for being selfish, but I've been impatient for a very long time. Did you know that eight years ago, I thought of secretly joining your mom, but she found out. She told me she would never forgive me if I did that. She asked me to live happily and share her blessings with everyone I meet. Only by doing that, she said, would people's blessings carry me into heaven when it's finally my turn. It was originally her mission—she wanted me to complete it for her. She promised to wait for me there, and once my mission is accomplished, we'd reunite in heaven. Then we'd continue our happy lives together forever. I promised her I'd fulfill her wish. And these past years in Paris, every day, I've shared the joy and blessings Manon left me with everyone I've encountered."

Lucas gently raised his hand, stopping Georgia from speaking, and continued quietly, "Sweetheart, by the time Mom passed away, you had already graduated from university and had been working for two years. Now, you've become quite the little rich lady! Your mom was always so proud of you. And now, look at how far you've come—I couldn't be prouder. Did you know that?

"When your mom left," Lucas said softly, "she took my heart along with her. For these past seven years, I've stayed in Paris because I was afraid she might forget her promise to me, and I worried that if I traveled too far, I wouldn't be able to find her again."

No matter how many tears Lucas wiped away, they continued to stream down Georgia's face. He looked at his daughter with an aching heart and said gently, "Georgia, your mom was a devout Christian. She always believed that her mission was to spread joy and blessings throughout the world. When she returned to the embrace of the Lord, I took over her mission. Now, sweetheart, I want to entrust this mission to you. Can you do this for us? This is your mother's and my heartfelt wish. Can you help us fulfill it?"

Georgia gazed at her father through eyes blurred with tears. "Will you and Mom wait for me in heaven? Can I still be your daughter there?"

Lucas felt his own tears overflow as he nodded emphatically. "Of course, sweetheart—of course! Your mom and I will be waiting for you in heaven. You'll always be our little angel and our darling daughter."

A relieved smile spread across Lucas's face, and he teasingly made a silly face at Georgia. "But no slacking off, young lady! Your mission won't be complete until your own grandchildren have grown up."

Georgia finally laughed, smiling through her tears. "Dad, I promise you. I'll share the happiness and blessings Mom gave to you, and that you gave to me, with everyone I meet. I promise I'll reunite with you both in heaven."

Lucas lovingly stroked his daughter's hair. "Sweetheart, when that day comes, I'd like to rest beside your mother. I've already bought the cemetery plot right next to hers."

Georgia looked at him sadly and scolded softly, "Dad, can we please not talk about this?"

Lucas immediately smiled apologetically, saying, "I'm sorry, sweetheart. Let's talk about something happier."

Spring sunlight filled the room, and a gentle breeze carried warmth into the hearts of father and daughter. Lucas began to tell Georgia about his experiences in Paris and the insights he had gained over the past half-year. As Georgia listened, she quickly pulled out her phone and started taking notes. Ivanov's quest for spiritual redemption, Sophia's vision of a heaven on earth, Jerry's profound compassion, Annie's journey of love . . . each story moved Georgia deeply, making her eager to interview these remarkable people. But at the moment, caring for her father was her most important desire. She wanted Lucas to walk joyfully toward the gates of heaven with her company.

Lucas then told Georgia about the young female artist from the East and her joke about finding ten people who would each split into ten paths.

Lucas said softly, "My dear daughter, though it started as just a joke, these three questions have truly taken root in my heart. I do believe Manon is waiting for me in heaven, yet what those two clergymen said has cast a lingering shadow of doubt upon my soul. Who exactly is God? Where does He reside? What is it that He desires from me? I understand each person may hold a unique answer to these questions. But as with the stories I've shared, even though people's beliefs differ greatly, their ultimate pursuits are remarkably alike. You're already a widely respected influencer, Georgia. Could you perhaps rally ten thousand people—or even a hundred thousand—to embark upon a hundred thousand different journeys to seek these answers?"

Georgia paused thoughtfully for a moment, then replied with determination, "Dad, I will. I want to find those answers as soon as possible, too."

Lucas gently patted his daughter's hand. "Sweetheart, truth matters more than time. What we truly seek are the answers about God. When you find them, no matter where I might be by then, just come and tell me."

Chapter 13

In the days that followed, Georgia stayed close by her father's side, sharing treasured memories and reliving all the beautiful moments they'd experienced together. Surprisingly, it was Lucas who became his daughter's emotional anchor, warming her fragile heart with his quiet strength.

Lucas firmly believed that love transcended life and death, bringing comfort and tranquility to the soul. With Georgia beside him, he reclaimed the inner peace that had eluded him for so long. He chose to forego further medical treatment, preferring instead that these valuable resources be given to others who needed them more—a final blessing to fellow patients. Though Georgia was heartbroken, she knew there was little more medicine could offer, and respecting her father's wishes was the greatest kindness and respect she could show to him.

As Lucas's physical health steadily declined, his faith grew stronger, anticipating a joyful reunion with his beloved wife. Each day, he radiated happiness, childlike and pure. Time passed like a gentle stream, and every morning Georgia brought fresh flowers, filling the room with their subtle fragrance, softening even the air around them.

Smiling gently, Georgia asked one day, "Dad, would you like to go back to our old house in Bellingham? Remember the beach in front of our home?"

Lucas sat up with excitement. "Do you mean you . . . ?"

"Yes, Dad," she said, smiling warmly, her eyes glistening with joyful tears. "I've bought back our old house in Bellingham. It's still as beautiful as we remember—even that silly message I scribbled under the stairs when I was little is still there."

Lucas burst into laughter. "Including that nasty remark about the neighbor's boy?"

Georgia laughed awkwardly along with him. "You always said that beach had the most beautiful sunsets in the world," she whispered softly as she arranged his bedside items.

"That's because I had you and Manon there," Lucas replied gently, eyes sparkling with happiness. His voice, though weak, was filled with longing. "I'll always remember the ocean breeze, the sand, and your mother's favorite seashells. We walked that beach nearly every day . . ."

"I'd like to take you back home," Georgia said tenderly, taking her father's hand in hers. "I've already arranged with a hospital in Bellingham to provide home visits and pain management."

Lucas placed his other hand on top of hers gratefully. "Thank you, sweetheart. Your understanding and support mean the world to me. The thought of quietly resting on the rocking chair, listening to your mother's favorite music, and gently drifting to sleep is exactly what I've dreamed of."

As he spoke, Lucas vividly pictured the old wooden rocking chair on their porch, gently creaking as it swayed, overlooking the familiar stretch of golden sand and the endless expanse of the tranquil blue sea.

Once in Bellingham, Lucas spent peaceful afternoons on the porch, swaying gently in the rocking chair while listening to soft music. On clear evenings, Georgia pushed his wheelchair along the beach. Just like when she was a little girl, she eagerly collected pretty shells and stones, running back to proudly show each new discovery to her father.

When rain fell, Lucas loved listening to the rhythmic patter on the window. Georgia knew he was thinking of her mother. Before Manon had passed away, she'd gently whispered to Lucas that the soft tapping of raindrops was her eternal message from heaven—each droplet carrying endless whispers of love and longing.

At night, sitting by the fireplace, Georgia softly shared stories of joyful times she'd spent with her mother. Their laughter echoed warmly throughout the old house. Georgia knew that these cherished memories were like fresh water, nourishing her father's soul.

Whenever Lucas's breathing became labored, Georgia would grasp his hand tightly, offering silent strength. Although doctors remained concerned about his declining health, they marveled each time at his extraordinary resilience and upbeat demeanor. Lucas's spirits remained remarkably steady; he greeted everyone with a gentle smile and sincere blessings each day.

When Lucas needed quiet time or rest, Georgia retreated to her study to chat with her fans. As an influencer adored by millions, she received thousands of messages daily, and she always tried her best to thoughtfully respond to her followers around the globe.

After thoughtful reflection one afternoon, Georgia posted a message online titled *The Heaven of Faith:*

"Usually, when people talk about faith, they immediately think of religion—each with its own gods and divine beings. But what about beliefs that aren't connected to gods at all? Environmentalism, human rights, labor rights, the pursuit of health and fitness, philanthropy—even the materialism so many chase—aren't these also forms of faith? Even the communism of the former Soviet Union can be considered a type of faith.

"Faith represents our spiritual pursuit, guiding us along life's journey. It's the compass pointing us toward our destination. Indeed, faith is the starting point for every path we choose, and different beliefs inevitably lead us down different roads.

"But what's at the end of that road? Why do we even need faith at all? Isn't it because we seek happiness? Each person defines happiness differently, giving rise to diverse beliefs. Thus, the destination of faith is the paradise of personal fulfillment—the moment someone achieves their happiness, they are living in their own heaven of belief.

"Yet, even those devoted to materialism or healthy living rarely feel they've reached paradise while alive. It's just as everyone dreams of captivating beauty, only to face emotional betrayals in real life.

"This brings up another question. Most of us spend our lives pursuing happiness. But will we ever reach that heaven we've imagined? Can anyone give me an answer?

"And if this all sounds complicated, let me put it in very American terms: every belief has its price. Are you willing to pay for yours? You're paying for something you hope to receive—you pay to get something, but if you don't keep paying for it continuously, what you want might only arrive after you've moved away.

"So, the final questions remain: Is God a being or a spirit? If we call God 'Him,' then who exactly is He? Where is He? What does He want me to do?

"Please, someone help me understand. I'm waiting online—and I really need your answers urgently."

Chapter 14

Georgia's followers numbered in the millions, spread all around the globe. After she posted her thoughts online, it immediately sparked waves of discussion. Like a mirror reflecting the world's complexities, it attracted countless responses, each revealing a unique understanding of faith or expressing personal confusion about life itself. Some replies were profound, some humorous, and others outright absurd.

A user calling himself the "Super Tech Nerd" jumped in first with a smirk: "Ha! God? I'm guessing He's the one fueling human technological progress. I mean, how else do you explain how fast everything's moving? These days, we're totally hooked on the internet. Autonomous platforms are everywhere, and humans? Well, we're starting to look kind of . . . unnecessary. If God really exists, then logic says He must be artificial intelligence—always among us, quietly watching. And what does He want most? For us to hurry up and wipe ourselves out."

Georgia chuckled to herself, shaking her head. "Is this guy secretly Elon Musk?"

Another reply from "Philosophical Chef" was equally surprising: "God is probably a cosmic chef, stirring the pot of the universe, mixing love and hate, hope and despair, while we're just dishes on his table. Who knows when we'll be served, or how we'll taste?"

Philosophical Chef's explanation was full of imagination, depicting a grand cosmic kitchen with humanity as ingredients in some universal recipe.

Georgia casually replied with a humorous emoji, rolling her eyes and muttering, "Oh my gosh, is this guy trying to imitate the Secretary of State?

Always associating everything with the dining table and what's on it?"

An anonymous poster called "Happy Ghostwriter" shared an amusing "shopping list for God":

God's Wish List:

1. *Endless praise and prayers (spiritual nourishment).*
2. *Occasional miracle displays (performance evaluations).*
3. *Absolute loyalty and faith (VIP membership).*

P.S.: No returns, no bad reviews accepted.

This list was amusing, as if even God had to deal with everyday "shopping troubles," just like mortal beings.

Georgia grinned, whispering under her breath, "Hmm . . . what is he, a supermarket owner or something?"

Another user named "Always Waiting for Take-out" replied, "God pops out from the delivery guy's thermal bag. Every time your favorite meal arrives, he tosses in a small surprise—a note saying, 'Keep being kind.'"

Georgia laughed softly, shaking her head. "This guy must be from China—where else would 99% of the world's food delivery drivers be?"

Someone nicknamed "Person You've Never Heard Of" wrote mysteriously: "God crawls out from your old TV set. When the static buzzes on the screen late at night, he stares at you silently, thinking, 'This kid is staying up late again.'"

Georgia exclaimed aloud, "Oh, come on—it's nighttime right now! This one must be Japanese."

A user known as "Looking Back from Afar" offered this perspective: "God jumps out of your unfinished puzzle. When you finally place the last piece, he appears and says, 'See? I'm the reason you feel accomplished.'"

Georgia nodded, hitting the *like* button. "This is

definitely someone who loves puzzles."

Then came a reply from "Forever Young Boy": "God is the neighbor kid sneaking into your fridge to drink your yogurt. But he's considerate enough to leave some behind, giving you a small daily blessing."

Georgia practically jumped from her chair, hands clutching her head in shock. "Oh my God! It must be Peter, the yogurt thief from next door—they moved away almost twenty years ago. How on earth is he still alive?"

She quickly typed a reply: "Wait, are you that yogurt-stealing kid? Aren't you afraid of being cursed?"

Reading through these colorful, even absurd replies, Georgia couldn't help but laugh. Initially, she'd only intended to find some spiritual comfort for her father; instead, she'd ignited an online carnival of faith conversations. This playful outburst allowed her to glimpse humanity's infinite variety in understanding faith and life. "Looks like this question really fired up everyone's imagination," she mused.

As her post gained popularity, increasingly imaginative replies flooded in, some deeply thoughtful, others delightfully ridiculous. Sitting at her computer, Georgia smiled, eyes sparkling with amusement and self-deprecating humor. She'd meant to toss a thoughtful pebble into the vast ocean of the internet but had unexpectedly triggered waves of joyous laughter. Those seemingly absurd answers glittered like iridescent bubbles in the sunlight, gently stirring her heart.

Deciding to shift gears, Georgia typed three fresh questions into this lively ocean, adopting a lighter, more playful tone. Carefully choosing each word, she wanted these new queries to strike more ripples:

"Hey everyone, let's shift gears and try something a little more 'American-style'," she began teasingly. "First things first—do you have your own kind of faith? Something that warms you up and keeps you strong, especially when the nights get quiet and long?"

Her question hit a nerve—it was asking, plain

and simple, what does faith really mean to each of us? And then the second question instantly appeared on the screen: "So, if such a belief truly existed, would you be willing to pay for it? Oh, don't misunderstand me—I'm not talking about spiritual sacrifice. I mean literally—money! For instance, would you donate to organizations associated with your faith, or perhaps buy merchandise featuring symbols of your belief?" This question is more practical, as it explores whether people are willing to pay a material price for their beliefs in real life.

She paused thoughtfully before typing out the final question, word by word: "Lastly, if your beliefs led you down an unconventional path—perhaps prompting you to abandon a lucrative career or a comfortable life, all for the sake of chasing your dreams or tirelessly pursuing a cause—would you regret that choice? Or is this exactly what you've been searching for, a path you'd follow joyfully, savoring each moment despite the uncertainty ahead?"

As these three questions hit the virtual sea, Georgia's screen once again erupted into lively responses.

"Of course, I have faith! Mine is that bag of chips by my bedside. Every night, when it's quiet and my stomach growls, it offers me the most tangible warmth and strength, whispering, 'Life is worth it—keep staying up!'"

"For me, faith is the ice cream in the freezer that never runs out. When the night grows quiet and I'm feeling down, just one spoonful sends sweetness straight to my soul, reminding me, 'Life may be tough, but don't be tough on yourself,' so I can smile again and face tomorrow."

"Pay for faith? Well, that depends if faith comes with a discount! If God said, "Be devout, and you'll get a special deal," I'd even buy my cat a matching faith-themed collar. But seriously, if that day ever comes, I'll probably need lessons on how to elegantly explain to the delivery person why all my packages are labeled 'Keys to the Gate of Wisdom' and 'Soul

Protection Charms!'"

"Oh gosh, reading this just gave me a brilliant business idea! We could start a 'Faith Bank,' where you deposit beliefs and withdraw discount coupons and deluxe faith-themed gift packages! Imagine, we'd all become life's winners by "saving faith and cashing out goodies" every day! And hey, if Wall Street big shots actually start paying for our beliefs, then surely America can be great again."

Glancing at the user ID—"TrumpFanNumber-300Million"—Georgia couldn't help but mutter, "Ugh . . . it's not actually him, is it?"

"In this world filled with countless choices, external voices often sway us. I chose to follow the call of my heart, leaving behind that high-paying job, and found an unprecedented peace. The path I've chosen is destined to be lonely and uncertain, yet it's guided by my soul."

The poster, whose username was "SunnyWorld-LostHeart," continued:

"The true value of life lies not in wealth or status but in how we realize our self-worth. I've taken a different path, abandoning a lucrative salary to chase my dreams and beliefs. Throughout this journey, I've deeply understood the true meaning and value of life. Real happiness, I've realized, comes from inner fulfillment, not material possessions. Hence, I have no regrets, because this choice represents my pursuit and realization of life's deeper meaning."

After reading this, Georgia felt deeply moved. She was reminded of the story Lucas had shared earlier about Alice and Jerry .

Some laughed joyfully, while others sank into quiet contemplation. Questions like these, posed online, always sparked curiosity and imagination. Maybe readers would soon drift off to sleep, but perhaps someday they'd awaken in the early morning, quietly reflecting upon their life's path.

Georgia sat quietly beside her computer, a gentle smile on her lips. She understood now that when people genuinely start picturing the life they wish for, faith quietly slips into their hearts. Each belief guides us along a distinct path, and in the end, everyone finds their own answer waiting—whether it turns out to be heaven or hell.

Chapter 15

Georgia's post, "Heaven and Faith," quickly went viral, shared countless times by her followers. Translated into numerous languages, it sparked global conversations. The three questions she posed afterward also became widely debated.

In Moscow, Russia, Ivanov sat quietly at his desk, gazing thoughtfully at the green buds outside his window. After a long silence, he typed his reply beneath Georgia's post:

"Once upon a time, somewhere on Earth, there was a group of people who dreamed of a world without exploitation, where everyone was respected and treated fairly. They envisioned creating a paradise here on Earth, believing deeply that the International would someday triumph. This was their faith. For this faith, they gave everything—including their lives. As one of them who still remains in this world, I just wanted to help those who have passed away to see if our sacrifices were worthwhile.

"You're right: if the ultimate goal of faith is paradise, few people can truly feel they're already living in heaven, unless they've cheated somehow. But can a cheater really call himself a true believer?

"Every believer's faith, before it's realized, might seem laughable to others. Yet if those others have their own beliefs, why would they mock someone else's? If they have none at all, what gives them the right to ridicule believers? All those who hold onto faith deserve respect because they're willing to carry burdens on behalf of those they love."

Quietly, Ivanov packed away his old uniform, rank insignia, and cap into an old-fashioned suitcase. His medals and certificates of honor were carefully placed in another bag. He reached into a hidden compartment in his drawer and removed a small box containing something from his past—inside, were items prepared for sacrifice during missions, known then as the "Keys to Paradise." After a final glance around his small apartment, he stepped outside and closed the door behind him.

At the Bolshevik headquarters in Moscow, Ivanov laid all his medals and awards neatly on an official's desk. From his bag, he took out his entire life savings and placed them atop the medals. Ignoring the puzzled gaze of the clerk, Ivanov stood at attention, solemnly saluting the Soviet flag and party emblem hanging on the wall. Then, picking up his suitcase, he turned without another word.

In the corridor, the party leader hurried after him, alarmed. "Ivan! Have you lost your mind? Why are you giving everything away? How will you live? You can talk to me!"

Without turning, Ivanov replied calmly, his gaze

fixed firmly ahead. "All my comrades have already gathered. I'm the only one left. I've waited thirty years. Now, I'm tired. I need rest. None of us regretted it—because it was our faith. I leave everything to you, hoping you'll rediscover what we once believed in. We were never meant to be the ones who lost our way."

Ivanov marched resolutely outside into the bright sunshine. Behind him, the elderly leader shook his head sadly, slowly disappearing into the building's shadows.

In Amman, Jordan, after prayers at the mosque, Fadi returned home, where his son Amin called him over to see Georgia's post online.

"Dad, this post says the endpoint of faith is heaven. But I feel happy right now. Does that mean we're already living in heaven?"

Fadi smiled warmly, gently patting his son's head. "Praise be to Allah, my son. Your happiness comes from His blessings. But we haven't reached heaven yet. In heaven, there's no hunger, no war, no discrimination—everyone lives in joy. We praise Allah because He teaches us kindness and love, enabling your current happiness. Yet many others still suffer from hunger and conflict. It's our duty to offer kindness and love to those who need it."

Amin tilted his head thoughtfully. "So, this is the cost of faith?"

Fadi laughed heartily. "You're basically correct to understand it this way, my boy. True believers always willingly sacrifice for their faith."

In Toronto, Canada, reading Georgia's post stirred deep reflection within Ivy, whose firm belief in environmental protection had always illuminated her path.

Turning toward Sophia, who lay ill in bed after contracting an illness during their Arctic research on melting glaciers, Ivy replied thoughtfully online:

"We all share one home. Protecting the earth's beauty and safeguarding the purity within our hearts have always been our life's mission.

"Your post makes me realize that protecting this blue planet we call home, and guarding the inner sanctuary of our beliefs, are profound expressions of life's purpose. Though we may not worship gods, our beliefs compel us to act—to remain steadfast in facing hardships and challenges.

"Just as we believe every effort to protect the environment adds strength to transform the world, every stirring of the heart on one's spiritual journey guides us toward greater self-understanding. Thank you for sharing these valuable insights. Your words reaffirm our conviction that if we live with faith and walk steadily forward, we'll eventually reach the heaven we each believe in."

In Edinburgh, Scotland, Annie, an elderly British woman, always wore a childlike smile—a face marked by years that left only peace and serenity. At the community center, she listened to volunteers reading Georgia's intriguing online post, *The Heaven of Faith*, an essay worthy of reflection.

"Oh, my dear John," she muttered cheerfully as she made her way home. "You've always been so patient, but you'll just have to wait a little longer."

Enjoying the warmth of the afternoon sun and the gentle breeze, Annie was suddenly halted by a young man who stepped directly into her path.

"I'm terribly sorry, ma'am, but this is a robbery," he said nervously. "I don't want to hurt you, but I need your wallet, please. Thank you for cooperating."

The young robber's eyes were anxious, even apologetic, revealing unexpected politeness despite his intentions.

Annie paused, quickly realizing this was no joke. Nodding gently, she replied, "Relax, son. There's no need to worry—I won't call the police. You can have my wallet, but please, could you let me keep my husband's photo inside it?"

The young man nodded apologetically.

As Annie reached for her wallet, she spoke softly to him. "Young man, take better care of yourself.

There's always someone in this world who loves you."

The young man said nothing as he took the wallet, pulled out a single twenty-pound note, and handed the wallet back to Annie before turning to run off.

But then, unexpectedly, after only a few steps, he tripped over a raised paving stone and fell hard onto the pavement. Annie hurried over, gently helping him up. "Are you alright, dear? Don't worry, I won't call the police."

Her words deepened his embarrassment. Without daring to meet her eyes, he quietly muttered a "Thank you" before running away again. Annie didn't say anything else, just watched kindly as the young man disappeared into the distance.

That evening, the young man returned to his neighborhood, to a shelter for the homeless. Under the dim streetlight, he glanced at a discarded newspaper he'd picked up earlier, which featured Georgia's viral post, *The Heaven of Faith*, and its widespread social impact. Deep in thought, he heard Annie's words echo in his ears. A comforting force seemed to soothe his restless soul, as the evening breeze gently brushed the dust off his long-sealed heart.

Chapter 16

In Irvine, California, USA, after reading Georgia's profound post exploring faith and the soul's ultimate destination, Alice found herself deeply moved. She decided to reply by sharing something of her own—an inspiring speech recently given by Mr. Lawrence, the principal at the school where she worked. Alice hoped Georgia might find comfort or inspiration in his words.

On the day of Mr. Lawrence's speech, both teachers and students had been profoundly touched. As Flora's mother, Alice herself had felt especially moved, and now she hoped Georgia might also share this beautiful message with others, if she liked.

The speech was titled "Faith and Happiness."

"Today is a beautiful, sunny day. One of our students, Flora, recently participated in a small fundraising event held at our school. She donated all her personal savings to help impoverished children in a certain region of Africa, hoping they might have the chance to attend school.

"Some of Flora's classmates warmly supported her, but others laughed and ridiculed her kindness. Heartbroken by their mockery, Flora cried. She believed kindness should be natural—why would anyone ridicule it? She didn't understand what she'd done wrong.

"When I heard about Flora's confusion, I felt troubled and deeply sorry. So, I invited everyone here today for a pizza party, to express my apology. The pizzas and drinks are on me.

"I organized this fundraising event after watching a television program about children in an impoverished region of Africa whose desperation at being unable to attend school deeply moved me. I felt compelled to help those children. More importantly, I wanted to inspire each of you to take action—to do something meaningful, not only for them but also for yourselves, even if it seems like just a small act of kindness. Thus, this fundraiser was born.

"Some classmates called Flora foolish, thinking a small fundraiser couldn't possibly change the world. They laughed because she had given everything she had. But Flora didn't let their skepticism stop her. She told me her father once said every effort counts, and even the smallest actions could change the world. Flora said she felt proud of her dad. And I'm sure her dad would be proud of her too—I know I certainly am.

"I invited everyone to help others because doing so allows each of you to discover your worth in this world. Acts of kindness elevate our souls. Your kindness shouldn't remain hidden—sharing kindness is the first step toward becoming noble individuals.

"Of course, giving should always match your capacity. You must first care for yourself before you can help others. But the amount you share should never be a reason for ridicule. Every small act of kindness brings a little more warmth and love into this world.

"I feel deeply proud of all our students because I know the seeds of kindness and love you plant today will bloom beautifully tomorrow. The purpose of education is to cultivate capable individuals. Only when you become capable can you truly help others. When kindness and love become our faith, each of us gains the power to transform the world. Even the smallest good deeds make the world better—so why not start today?

"I once read that a person without faith is like a body without a soul—wandering through the world but never truly experiencing human warmth and light. Faith is the guiding lantern of our spirits, illuminating our paths.

"Only those with faith understand reverence because they recognize that we cannot simply do whatever we please. A person who reveres others respects their parents, developing good character and behavior. Students who revere their teachers gain knowledge and a deeper understanding of the world. Citizens who revere the law achieve success and happiness in society.

"Most importantly, those who hold reverence in their hearts also feel gratitude. At home, they appreciate their parents' love and care. At school, they are thankful for the guidance of teachers and the companionship of classmates. In society, they cherish community efforts and treasure every blessing they receive. Those who understand gratitude experience genuine family bonds, friendships, and love.

"A grateful person will have a life filled with happiness and sunshine. In contrast, those who lack gratitude always feel that their parents, school, friends, or even society owes them something. Such individuals can never truly be happy—their hearts remain clouded by resentment."

What Alice didn't know was that after she shared Principal Lawrence's speech online, Georgia liked and reposted it, drawing hundreds of thousands of reactions. Among those deeply touched was Flora's father, Jerry.

One evening, Alice and Flora were completing a crossword puzzle together at home when the phone rang. Alice was startled to hear Jerry's anxious voice on the line.

"Alice, I'm so sorry. When Flora needed me most, I wasn't there. I read your post, and I've already called Principal Lawrence to personally thank him for everything he's done for Flora."

Alice felt her heart swell with emotion, tears silently running down her cheeks.

Not hearing any response, Jerry asked anxiously, "Alice, can you hear me? Alice?"

Finally, Alice burst into tears. "Jerry, you're such

a jerk! I told you not to disturb my life, but does that mean you should never call?"

Jerry hastily replied, "I'm so sorry . . ."

"No," Alice interrupted, sobbing softly. "I should be apologizing—I should've called you sooner."

Jerry, confused and worried, urgently said, "Honey, what happened? Please tell me—whatever it is, we'll handle it together."

Wiping away her tears, Alice quietly asked, "Jerry, do you still love me? Do you still love our family?"

Joy surged in Jerry's voice. "Honey, have you forgiven me? I've always loved you—I've always loved our family."

Alice then told Jerry about their time in Paris and meeting an elderly gentleman named Lucas. She'd shared Jerry's story with Lucas, who deeply admired Jerry's dedication. Lucas reminded Alice of something Jerry often said: if the world lost kindness and love, it would become a living hell. Lucas added their home was the same—if everyone gave their home a little love every day, each home would become their own heaven.

Jerry was ecstatic. "Honey, I must thank this Mr. Lucas. He truly is our angel!"

Alice smiled warmly. "That's exactly what I told him."

Turning toward Flora, Alice softly called, "Flora, come here—your dad wants to talk to you."

The little girl, nervously eavesdropping nearby, saw the smile and tears of happiness on her mother's face. Her own tears couldn't help but fall, blending into her flower-like smile.

Chapter 17

On a sunlit morning, Lucas sat quietly in a rocking chair on the front porch, having just finished the breakfast his daughter had lovingly prepared. Wrapped comfortably in the blanket his wife, Manon, used to cherish, he listened softly to her favorite songs playing in the background. His gaze wandered out across the bay, where sailboats drifted gently like distant memories, and with a tender smile on his lips, he whispered quietly to himself.

In the study, Georgia watched her father's peaceful silhouette through the window, tears mingling in her eyes, filled with gratitude and bittersweet affection. Suddenly, a notification popped up on her computer: a friend request from a prominent online influencer named "A Priest Searching for Lost Lambs." This user had millions of followers, and intriguingly, his profile identified him as a Cardinal.

Georgia immediately accepted the request and politely greeted His Eminence. He gently requested a voice call, apologizing politely that, due to his advanced age, he found it difficult to coordinate his vision and typing.

Georgia immediately initiated the call.

A deep, comforting voice, filled with warmth, came through the speakers: "May I call you Georgia?"

"Of course," she replied.

The Cardinal continued, "A friend forwarded your post, *Heaven and Faith,* to me. I read it attentively and was deeply moved by your profound insight. The questions you posed afterward are equally thought-provoking. Now that we're connected as friends, would you mind sharing the story behind those questions?"

"I don't mind at all," Georgia said calmly. "My parents met thirty-six years ago in Paris and loved each other deeply. Eight years ago, my mother passed away. Following her wishes, my father buried her in Paris, beside my grandparents. Since then, he's stayed in Paris, faithfully honoring her memory. My mother asked my father to live happily and share her blessings with everyone he meets, promising she'd wait for him in heaven. He worries she'll forget their promise, so he settled in Paris and visits her grave every week to remind her. He's old now, and I'd tried to bring him back to the United States where I could care for him in the past seven years, but he always refuses. He says when my mother left, his heart went with her."

Georgia's voice trembled, tears falling silently as she spoke.

Sensing her distress, the Cardinal gently comforted her: "My dear child, our life is never just one journey. Each ending is simply another beginning."

Georgia nodded gratefully. "My parents always believed this deeply. They taught me that only noble, pure souls enter heaven, while polluted souls sink deeper into darkness, ultimately falling into the abyss of hell."

Moved by her words, the Cardinal softly praised the Holy Mother.

Embarrassed, Georgia admitted softly that her parents were both Protestant Christians.

He chuckled warmly, "Child, the Holy Mother or God desires only that our journey ends in heaven. Whether you arrive dressed in pajamas or an evening gown matters not at all."

Georgia then shared another story. "Last autumn, my father met a young artist who revealed a strange dream she'd been carrying for half a year. In her dream, she saw a holy church and heard a powerful voice commanding her to share it with the world, cryptically adding, 'You will understand in due time.' She painted this vivid dream, certain such a church didn't exist anywhere on earth. Being Eastern and without religious belief, she didn't know what to do. But she saw my father's devotion and kindness, and chose him to be the first to see her painting. My father was amazed, calling it a miracle. Though he, too, didn't quite understand what that meant, convinced the voice she heard was the voice of God."

The Cardinal gently interrupted, curiosity in his voice: "Do you have this painting? Could you show it to me?"

Georgia said, "Just a moment, please," then quickly located the image on her computer and sent it to the Cardinal.

After a brief pause, his voice returned warmly: "This is indeed miraculous. This structure resembles the coronets worn by the nuns in our convents—holy, beautiful, and destined to become a truly magnificent monastery. This monastery certainly has never appeared on earth; its beauty is unforgettable."

Knowing this wasn't the story's end, he prompted gently, "And then?"

Georgia sighed softly. "My father excitedly took the painting to his local church, eager to share this miracle. But the priest dismissed it, claiming miracles were merely human fantasies. He said he'd served God for decades but had never heard His voice—so how could anyone else?"

The Cardinal coughed lightly.

"Your Eminence, are you alright?" Georgia asked worriedly.

"I'm fine, please continue."

Georgia proceeded gently, "Suddenly, my father became very anxious. My mother's promise to him was that they'd reunite in heaven. If there was no God, would heaven even exist? The young artist suggested perhaps the image belonged to another faith."

"Yes, quite right," the Cardinal responded from the other end, his voice carrying a faint, unmistakable note of embarrassment.

"So, she accompanied my father to the Vatican."

"Oh?" the Cardinal reacted, embarrassed. "Do continue."

Georgia continued, her voice shaking slightly, "In a private meeting there, my father repeated the dream and showed the painting. The priest told him dreams were merely reflections of our personal obsessions, and he had been a clergyman for decades, always advising people to let go of their obsessions and embrace life."

Another cough interrupted her.

"Your Eminence, perhaps some water?" Georgia said anxiously. Quietly, she revealed, "My father is seriously ill. He hid this from me for a long time, but he doesn't have much time left. He desperately wants answers: Does God exist? Is there heaven? Who is God? Where is He? What does He want from us? From last autumn to this spring, he asked everyone he met until illness confined him to his bed. These are the stories behind my questions."

Georgia's voice quivered again.

Moved deeply, the Cardinal responded softly, providing gentle clarity: "My child, your story touches my heart profoundly. It just so happens I have answers for you . . .

"I can assure you with certainty that both heaven and hell exist. Each one of us requires a soul to discern right from wrong and to guide us through life. Your mother and father were right: heaven only accepts souls that are pure and noble. Once tainted, the soul gradually descends toward the abyss of hell. Therefore, when we recognize that our souls have become corrupted, we must seek redemption. Confession is merely the first step toward salvation; the true redemption of the soul lies in making love and kindness the core of our inner world. Your mother spoke truthfully—when you share kindness and blessings with everyone you meet in life, your soul becomes elevated and purified. The blessings that return to you from those you've blessed are what ultimately raise your soul to heaven."

Georgia asked cautiously, "Your Excellency, can you please tell me the answer?"

The Cardinal replied warmly, "Yes, my child. I am here today precisely to give you the answer. Rest assured, God has always been with us.

"But who ever said God needs to be observed by humans like some kind of pet, obligated to respond to every single prayer? Billions of people are alive every day—how could He possibly manage it all?

"Every life that enters this world embarks on a journey of spiritual growth and refinement. Every human soul is like a fundamental particle within God's spiritual universe. The trials and experiences each soul endures are, in essence, God's own process of spiritual evolution.

"Through this journey, souls that become purified, more noble and holy, return into God's embrace, embarking again on the next chapter of their existence.

"You can understand this concept more clearly by referencing the multidimensional theories that scientists are currently exploring. Conversely, corrupted souls sink into lower dimensions. In such dark worlds, even kings can be slaughtered. Only those who cling to the last remnants of love and kindness can redeem themselves. When every trace of humanity in that realm is extinguished, it becomes a genuine abyss of hell—thus losing its very reason for existence."

The Cardinal's voice was deep and comforting, yet Georgia felt chills running down her spine.

He continued gently, "My child, having reached this point, the answer should be clear now . . .

"Who is God? God is the one who loves you most! Because God loves humanity, He wishes everyone to feel loved. Therefore, He takes the form of those who love you most, appearing by your side to offer you His blessings.

"And where is God? God resides within your

heart! Because God loves you, He naturally becomes the person you hold dearest. As long as you still have someone you love within your heart, your humanity—or divine nature—will never be fully lost, and self-redemption remains possible.

"What does God desire for you? Simply your happiness and joy! Since God loves you, He naturally wishes you happiness and fulfillment. Only when you feel truly happy and content can you extend blessings to everyone you encounter throughout your life. Through this spiritual refinement, souls become increasingly noble and sacred, ultimately achieving transcendence."

At that moment, the wind chime on the porch gently rang, and a pleasant voice came through. The chime had been bought by Georgia's mother, and it was one reason her father always loved sitting in the rocking chair there.

The Cardinal sighed softly, warmth and compassion in his voice, "Georgia, let's pause our conversation here. Please, go and tell Lucas that Manon will surely be waiting for him—right there, in heaven."

With that, the Cardinal signed off.

Georgia sprang up joyfully and stepped out onto the porch, her heart dancing with happiness—until she suddenly froze at the sight of her father. Lucas sat peacefully in his rocking chair, a gentle smile frozen in sleep. His music player had fallen from his grip, his hands relaxed.

Georgia gently knelt beside Lucas, resting her head against her father's chest as tears streamed down her cheeks.

The wind chimes softly jingled again. A distant ship's whistle echoed across the sea, mingling with the cheerful laughter of children running along the beach.

Holding Lucas's cold hand, Georgia cried for a long time, unable to tell how much time had passed. Remembering the Cardinal's words, she leaned closer to her father, softly whispering the answers he had shared with her just moments ago.

As she uttered the Cardinal's final blessing, Georgia suddenly froze. A realization flashed through her mind like lightning—she replayed the entire conversation clearly in her thoughts. Throughout her exchange with the Cardinal, she had only ever mentioned "mother" and "father," never once saying their names, Manon or Lucas.

At that very moment, the wind chimes rang gently once more, and a flock of geese called out as they gracefully soared across the distant horizon.

Chapter 18

Georgia sat quietly on the rocking chair on the porch, watching the distant sails drift gently across the horizon. The melodious wind chimes swayed softly, soothing her heart. Slowly, the sadness in her eyes turned into resolute determination. Gazing at the clouds floating serenely overhead, she rose to her feet.

Her sadness stemmed from her father's passing, yet her newfound strength came from the promise she had made to him. She had vowed to live joyfully, carrying forward the blessings her mother had given her father, which he, in turn, entrusted to her—to share warmth and kindness with everyone she met on life's journey.

Georgia knew her parents were now reunited in heaven. Strangely, every record of her conversation with the Cardinal had mysteriously vanished, and his online ID was nowhere to be found. Whenever she tried to write anything explicitly mentioning God, the words simply wouldn't appear. Yet every detail of their conversation remained vivid in her memory. Georgia understood—it was her parents' profound love for the world that had earned them divine favor. Now, she knew exactly what she must do.

Recalling her father's stories—beginning with the dream of the young Eastern artist, followed by Lucas's accounts of spiritual redemption, and finally, the clear voice from her own memory—Georgia finally understood the meaning behind the voice in her dream: "You will understand." The dream just to guide people toward finding heaven had been merely a signpost, guiding souls onto the path to heaven.

Georgia knew that whenever it came to writing anything explicitly involving the word "God," she simply couldn't bring herself to do it. Georgia transformed her dialogue with the Cardinal into an exchange with an anonymous internet user. She published a post titled *The Path to Heaven.*

In her post, Georgia thanked thousands of online followers for their previous responses. She explained candidly that the questions she had asked online were initially meant to help her father find his spiritual path. She shared Lucas's story for seeking the path to heaven, the personal quest behind the questions, and recounted the profound dialogue she'd had with the anonymous user. Lastly, she expressed gratitude that she had conveyed these answers to her father before he had passed.

Georgia publicly thanked the anonymous user, expressing her firm belief that her parents were now happily reunited in heaven.

The power of the internet was astonishing; Georgia's heartfelt post quickly spread worldwide. Initially, readers were deeply moved by the enduring love between Lucas and Manon. Soon, however, curiosity shifted toward the anonymous user "Seeker of Lost Sheep," whose insightful responses resonated deeply with countless souls. When people tried to follow or contact this mysterious figure, they found no trace of him. The search intensified rapidly, from hundreds to thousands, and eventually millions joined the global quest.

Georgia became increasingly frustrated by endless inquiries. Of course, she knew exactly what had happened—even the username had been created by her—but she found herself completely unable to explain it. As her post was translated into various languages and spread worldwide, the number of people searching for the mysterious "Seeker of Lost Sheep" surpassed ten million. This widespread curiosity brought even greater attention to Georgia's post, *The Path to Heaven*, drawing more and more people into the search.

Occasionally, someone considered impersonating this wise figure, but such attempts inevitably failed. Ordinary people simply couldn't convincingly portray a sage, and a true wise man would never engage in such deceitful acts. This impossibility only intensified everyone's curiosity about his true identity. The more elusive he became, the more eager people were to find him.

Then one day, an online commenter casually remarked, "Could it be that this mysterious 'he' is actually Him?"

Instantly, the entire online world fell into stunned silence, reminiscent of when a comet had collided with Jupiter years earlier. This suggestion resonated deeply with many people's unspoken hopes. Soon, religious organizations around the globe started to claim this "miracle" as their own. This led to further astonishment—how could diverse religions and differing faiths suddenly unite in agreement over this one question? Could it be that the answer provided by this mysterious figure was truly the ultimate truth?

Georgia had never anticipated the situation developing in this manner. As curiosity about the mysterious figure grew, so too did acceptance of the answers he had given. Meanwhile, the love story of Lucas and Manon became widely celebrated around the world.

In Tokyo, Japan, in a bustling corner of this modern city, Mr. Yamamoto, whom Lucas had once driven around and was renowned for his sharp business acumen, also read Georgia's *The Path to Heaven.*

"Lucas is gone? Such a pity. He was truly wise."

Moved deeply by the philosophical reflections and exploration of life's meaning, Mr. Yamamoto sat quietly on the tatami floor of his study. Gazing out at Tokyo's glittering skyline, ripples gently stirred in his heart, as tears quietly filled his eyes.

His son, Shinichi, returned home and was startled by his father's emotional state. "Father, what's wrong? Why are you suddenly crying?" he asked cautiously, with concern.

Gently wiping his tears, Mr. Yamamoto offered a faint, bittersweet smile. "Ah, Shinichi, I just read a post online that reminded me vividly of your grandparents. Every Sunday morning, they faithfully climbed the mountain path to the ancient temple to burn incense and pray, believing it brought peace and happiness to our family. Yet here I am, their son, barely managing to go once a month. It fills me with shame."

His words echoed profound longing for his departed parents.

After a pause, he continued, "Someone once asked me about faith and heaven. At the time, I couldn't clearly answer. But now, I desperately wish to understand—especially when considering my eventual fate, wondering where my soul might go."

Observing his son's confusion, Mr. Yamamoto laughed wryly. "Shinichi, your grandfather was a businessman, as we both are. Businessmen must pursue certainty and control, guiding outcomes toward predictability. So, the critical question is—can I secure a ticket to heaven?"

His voice carried a hint of self-mockery.

At this point, Mr. Yamamoto couldn't help but chuckle once again, a laugh mixed with a touch of bitterness, a dash of cunning humor, and a measure of acceptance. "So, Shinichi, tomorrow let's put aside those dull business discussions. Come with me to the ancient temple on the mountain. You must understand, we're not simply going there to seek blessings—we're making a long-term investment, securing tickets for our family's entrance into paradise. Opportunity only favors those who are prepared, and sincerity is what ensures success. Perhaps Buddha, noticing our heartfelt devotion, might even set aside a few VIP tickets for us!"

In Paris, France, in a serene suburban cemetery, Lucas's cherished black car was respectfully displayed by the entrance, named "Vehicle for Sharing Love and Kindness" by cemetery management. A bronze plaque recounted Lucas and Manon's enduring love story. Visitors, moved by their tale, laid flowers before the car.

Inside the graveyard, Georgia stood silently before her parents' gravestone, tears gently falling, mingling softly with her wistful, affectionate smile.

Chapter 19

Georgia had never imagined her post, *The Path to Heaven,* would create such immense ripples across the internet, resonating profoundly with countless people worldwide. Beyond her initial astonishment, a surge of indescribable joy welled within her heart.

She realized that amidst the vast sea of humanity, countless souls quietly sought their life's ultimate destination, just as she did. This shared resonance made her feel gently propelled by an invisible force, carried along by the currents of collective consciousness.

One afternoon, Georgia received a call from the East. It was An Ting, a dear friend she'd made while studying abroad in China several years prior. Back then, An Ting had been Georgia's dance instructor, and Georgia had taught her English. Their relationship had quickly blossomed into an intimate, sisterly bond.

Knowing Georgia's personality and family situation intimately, An Ting directly expressed her concern after reading the post. "Georgia, I'm so sorry—I only just heard about your father. Is there anything I can do to help?"

Georgia's heart warmed with gratitude. "Thank you, An Ting. Everything that needed doing is already done. How are you doing lately? And how are your two kids?"

At the mention of her children, An Ting's voice bubbled over with joy, childlike in its pure delight.

"I'm so sorry I missed your wedding," Georgia said gently. "I'd love to visit you and meet your family in China soon. Would that be okay?"

An Ting let out an ecstatic shout. "Really? That's

fantastic! Of course, you're welcome! My husband and I would be thrilled to have you."

Excitedly, An Ting continued, "My husband is planning to invest in a wedding-themed photography park covering around 200 hectares, entirely themed around love and romance. Maybe you could give us some ideas when you visit. And when you get married someday, we'll reserve the entire park exclusively for your wedding."

A thought stirred in Georgia's heart. "Will your husband's planned park include a chapel?"

An Ting laughed somewhat sheepishly. "Well, you know how it is here in China."

Georgia smiled apologetically. "I understand. But doesn't a Western-style wedding deserve a proper chapel?"

An Ting immediately perked up. "Exactly! Do you have any suggestions?"

Georgia spoke animatedly, "You remember the dream chapel at the beginning of *The Path to Heav-*

en? That beautiful chapel was envisioned by a young Chinese artist, who dreamed and painted it. When she traveled to Paris for her exhibition, my father Lucas was the first person she told. Today, you've mentioned your husband's wedding-themed park—but it has no chapel design yet. An Ting, wouldn't it be incredible if this dream-born chapel came to life exactly where the dream began?"

Fully persuaded, An Ting exclaimed, "Georgia, you're brilliant! I'll discuss this immediately with my husband. If we can make this happen, it would truly be a miracle. Georgia, do you have that drawing from the dream? Send it to me now."

Moments later, An Ting received the stunning image of a chapel standing gracefully upon a hillside. She knew instantly that anyone marrying there would cherish the memory forever.

That evening, when An Ting's husband, Jiang Dong, returned home from work, she eagerly brought up the topic and showed him the drawing from the dream to further persuade him. Jiang Dong took the drawing, his eyes sparkling with immediate admiration. After reading Georgia's post, *The Path to Heaven,* he was deeply intrigued but knew getting approval for such a chapel would be challenging.

Seeing her husband lost in thought while holding the chapel drawing, An Ting quietly poured a cup of tea and silently handed it to him.

Suddenly, Jiang Dong's eyes misted, tears forming at their edges.

Alarmed, An Ting asked gently, "Honey, what's the matter?"

Gazing distantly, Jiang Dong spoke slowly. "I was just remembering my mother, thinking about my childhood. It hit me—I never did anything substantial for her. It was always her silently sacrificing herself for our family. She's been gone for thirty years, and my heart aches with regret that nothing can soothe."

His voice trembled softly with deep longing and remorse.

An Ting tenderly clasped his hand, silently comforting him.

After a moment, Jiang Dong sighed deeply, his voice choked with emotion. "You know, some people sacrifice everything for their beliefs. When I was little, my family was poor. We couldn't afford doctors or medicine. Whenever I fell ill, my mother would hold me tightly, kneeling before her shrine, gently pressing her forehead to mine. Only later did I understand—she hoped to take my illness onto herself. And then I'd be well again, in no time. She was so foolishly selfless—but she loved me more than anything in this world."

Finally unable to hold back, Jiang Dong broke down into audible sobs, tears streaming down his face. "This is my mother, who is always willing to sacrifice everything she has for me. My mother lives forever in my heart! I've often wondered what I could do to truly honor her memory and comfort her spirit."

He held up the chapel drawing decisively, his

voice firm with resolve. "This—this is it. Thank you, my dear."

Shortly after, with Georgia's help, An Ting reached out to Wei Yixin, the young Chinese artist, through Lucas's contacts. At the time, Wei Yixin was touring Guangxi province in her RV, gathering inspiration. Thanks to Lucas and Georgia's connection, they quickly agreed to license the chapel design.

Days later, Jiang Dong sat nervously across from a government official meticulously reviewing the architectural details. Pointing at the chapel sketch, the official asked sternly, "What's this?"

Jiang Dong nodded eagerly, smiling anxiously. "It's a wedding chapel—essential for our park's wedding photography and ceremonies. Without a chapel, our park would be like a body without a soul."

The official studied Jiang Dong intently, then carefully examined the drawing again. After a thoughtful pause, he reached decisively for the official stamp and firmly approved the design. Hand-ing back the documents, he simply said, "Do a good job."

A wave of relief washed over Jiang Dong as the stamp landed decisively. With heartfelt gratitude, he grasped the official's hand in both of his own, bowing repeatedly and earnestly thanking him.

"Thank you so much, sir! Truly, thank you!"

Chapter 20

Time passed swiftly, and soon the park was completed. Jiang Dong eagerly and passionately prepared for the grand opening ceremony, awaiting numerous distinguished guests. The wedding-themed park was about to welcome the public.

The wedding chapel's spire soared high into the clouds, reminiscent of an angel's staff. Carefully sculpted with graceful lines, its pinnacle gleamed brilliantly in the sunlight, as if guiding souls through the heavens, carrying love to the far reaches of the universe.

From the outside, the chapel resembled a holy goddess's mantle gently spreading across the earth—soft yet dignified. Countless intricate white stones and glass panels intertwined seamlessly, embodying both traditional solemnity and modern transparent beauty. Gentle rays of sunlight pierced through clouds, softly illuminating the sacred ground. Every ray of sunlight was delicately captured and gradually released by the reflective surfaces, cloaking the entire chapel in a delicate golden shimmer, like a veil of the finest golden sand, radiating romantic and divine brilliance.

Stepping into the chapel, beneath its soaring dome, visitors were greeted by beautifully arranged seating and refined decor. Each carefully crafted detail and every ray of light within the space seemed to fill the atmosphere with profound love and boundless hope. Each spoken vow and musical note gently resonated, echoing pure love deeply within every heart.

This chapel, born from the young artist's vision, would witness countless joyful unions, becoming an everlasting sweet memory cherished in the hearts of those married there.

At the ribbon-cutting ceremony, Jiang Dong and

his wife An Ting, along with Georgia and the young artist Wei Yixin, stood together with numerous internet celebrities, adding glamour to the grand celebration. Visitors flowed continuously into the park, immersed in its magical world filled with love and romance.

Meanwhile, at the rear of the bustling crowd, a white couple wearing elegant hats slowly walked hand-in-hand into the park, blending quietly into the stream of visitors.

Above them, the sky stretched clear and deep-blue, wisps of white clouds drifting lazily across the horizon. Sunlight fell gently upon their figures, wrapping them in a soft golden glow. As a flock of white doves flew gracefully overhead, they slowly lifted their gaze, and beneath their hats, their faces gently came into view.

"So, this is God's perspective," Lucas softy whispered.

Lucas and Manon both wore radiant, gentle smiles.

Epilogue

A year earlier, during the Christmas and New Year holidays, a father and his teenage daughter, who loved drawing, sat chatting in their study. The father shared the journey of the artist Wei Yixin in Europe with his sixteen-year-old daughter.

After listening attentively, she asked, "Dad, does hard work always pay off?"

The question wasn't easy to answer. After careful thought, he chose honesty: "In your studies, yes—hard work will always pay off. Even if your IQ was half someone else's, you'd simply need to spend twice as long studying. Many things in life depend on luck, but education is the exception. If you genuinely commit yourself, your efforts will surely bear fruit."

He continued gently, "Every effort you make now raises the starting point for your future. Once you leave school and enter society, you must continue to work hard, nurturing not just knowledge, but also emotional intelligence. Work diligently, cultivate sincere friendships, generously help others, and deeply cherish every opportunity. But outside education, hard work alone might not guarantee immediate rewards—you'll also need good luck. Yes, some people are favored by fortune, but clearly, we aren't among them. Yet, gradually, you'll realize that your dedication to learning enhances your self-worth. Hard work brings broad recognition, sincere friendships offer valuable support, kindness opens more doors, and gratitude turns opportunities into success. Over time, your persistent efforts will attract luck until you create your own fortune."

After thinking for a moment, she asked, "If hard

work is the beginning and process of my life, what about the end? How will my story conclude?"

It was a profound question. Reflecting carefully, her father answered from another perspective: "Everyone is the protagonist of their own life story, while those around us are merely supporting characters. Your life is like a journey on your own train. People board and depart at different stations; some ride briefly alongside you before going their separate ways, while others stay for the entire journey. I don't know why strangers board the same train, but from the moment you're born, your unique story unfolds. Whether you become a princess or remain Cinderella partly depends on your choices—but ultimately, some outcomes must be left to God."

Quietly, his daughter asked again, "And you, Dad? What role have you played in your life story?"

Her question slightly embarrassed him. With a wry smile, he softly admitted, "Maybe I'm just a clown performing on the street corner—someone people rarely stop to notice, even for a moment. There's no applause, but still, I keep dancing and performing my heart out."

He gestured gently, urging her to let him finish: "Even if my performances rarely earn praise, there are still rewards. Whenever I picture the warm glow of our home's front door, your mother's gentle smile under the lamplight, and you and your sister's sweet laughter, it gives me the strength to dance even harder."

Emotionally, his daughter blurted, "You're not a clown! You're our family's greatest hero—you can't say that about yourself!"

He tenderly stroked her hair. "Thank you, sweetheart. I don't steal, cheat, or hurt anyone, so your dad is a decent person. When I was young, I lacked manners. One day, your grandfather asked me, 'If someone were pointing a knife or a gun at you, you'd manage to speak politely, wouldn't you?' I was left speechless. Your grandfather taught me as long as we don't steal, cheat, or harm others, we are good people. Good parents all around the world form countless happy families, dedicating the best moments of their lives to loved ones. To their children, they're true heroes. So, I willingly accept my role. All I need to do is keep striving. In our life stories, applause and cheers belong to others. Praise is fleeting, but happiness—that is the eternal pursuit on our life's journey."

After a thoughtful pause, she asked, "Dad, can I write a novel about the young artist's story?"

Surprised, he asked her reason for wanting this.

She explained, "Many people's stories are fascinating. Combining them could itself be extraordinary."

Her father replied gently, saying they'd first need Wei Yixin's permission.

A month later, she outlined the story and sighed to her father, "Dad, my Chinese isn't good enough. Could you help write the Chinese version?"

After hearing this, her father was momentarily speechless, but as a father trying to encourage his child's efforts, he could only smile and say, "Sweetheart, it's okay! Daddy's English only goes as far as 'hello' and 'nice weather today.' But this is a story about faith—do you think a Chinese version would be meaningful?"

His daughter rolled her eyes and replied, "Dad, in my story, faith isn't just about religion. I do believe it's meaningful. You once told me that as long as we try our best, we won't have regrets. Since we're going to do this anyway, why not make it as good as possible?"

Her father could only smile wryly and say, "All right, then—let's work hard together."

And thus, this book came into existence, in both English and Chinese editions.

In October 2023, Wei Yixin's painting *Sunset* was exhibited at the Louvre Museum in France. On February 13, 2024, her artwork *Sunset* was invited to participate in the Grand Palais Art Exhibition in Paris, organized by the French Ministry of Culture and the Réunion des Musées Nationaux.

The Return and Rise of impressionism a Century later–Wei Yixin's "Sunset"

As Camille Verdier in *Factstory of Agence France-Presse* commented about Wei Yixin's painting, "This marks the return and rise of Impressionism a century later. Her paintings are not only a display of exquisite techniques, but also a tribute and continuation of traditional art."

– October 26, 2023

About the Author

Emily Minjun Chung was born in January 2008 and is a Chinese Canadian. At the age of one, she immigrated to Canada with her parents and settled by the seaside in Surrey, British Columbia.

At age five, she began attending White Rock Christian Academy. Since early childhood, she has loved reading and drawing. Her abundant energy and insatiable curiosity often made it challenging for people around her to keep up as she explored the world with enthusiasm. She often says she's lucky to have "the best dad in the world," and her dad always rolls his eyes and replies, "That's only because you have the best grandpa in the world."

Emily began learning French, German, and Japanese when she was five. For four consecutive years, she studied as a guest student in local schools in Austria and Japan—a move her parents made simply to help burn off her endless energy.

At the age of eleven, she fell in love with writing and began publishing her work online. The praise and support from readers and fans always gave her an energy boost that could last an entire day. Back then, she wrote about stories from a little girl's dreams—stories she created mainly for herself, finding joy in the process of creation.

At twelve, she moved to China with her parents due to her father's work and has since been attending BASIS International School of Guangzhou. At school, her writing and artistic talents have been praised by both teachers and classmates. What she cherishes most, however, is the joy that comes from friendship and being truly seen and appreciated.